STRATEGIC IMPASSE

"Damned if you do; damned if you don't" voices the strategic impasse the USA finds itself in today. Liberal interventionism and globalization—the two pillars of the international system—seem not to work. Explaining the inability of Western powers to enact wise initiatives, Corradi explores the de-coupling of political systems: we are connected with each other but disconnected from policy makers. The paradox of increased connectivity and collective disengagement sets a perverse dynamic between publics and elites, with a serious impact on world affairs. Corradi analyzes the social bases of present dilemmas and how incipient decline can be managed, and paralysis overcome.

Dr. Juan E. Corradi is Emeritus Professor of Sociology at New York University and the author of the book, *South of the Crisis: Latin American Perspectives on the Late Capitalist World* (Anthem Press, 2010). As a native Latin American teaching in the USA, his work in cultural sociology has informed his scholarship on world affairs for four decades.

STRATEGIC IMPASSE

Social Origins of Geopolitical Disarray

Juan E. Corradi

Routledge
Taylor & Francis Group
NEW YORK AND LONDON

First published 2019
by Routledge
711 Third Avenue, New York, NY 10017

and by Routledge
2 Park Square, Milton Park, Abingdon, Oxon, OX14 4RN

Routledge is an imprint of the Taylor & Francis Group, an informa business

© 2019 Taylor & Francis

The right of Juan E. Corradi to be identified as the author of this work has been asserted by him in accordance with sections 77 and 78 of the Copyright, Designs and Patents Act 1988.

All rights reserved. No part of this book may be reprinted or reproduced or utilised in any form or by any electronic, mechanical, or other means, now known or hereafter invented, including photocopying and recording, or in any information storage or retrieval system, without permission in writing from the publishers.

Trademark notice: Product or corporate names may be trademarks or registered trademarks, and are used only for identification and explanation without intent to infringe.

Library of Congress Cataloging-in-Publication Data
Names: Corradi, Juan E., author.
Title: Strategic impasse : social origins of geopolitical disarray / by Juan E. Corradi.
Description: New York, NY : Routledge, 2018. | Includes index.
Identifiers: LCCN 2018011341| ISBN 9781138212565 (hb) | ISBN 9781138212572 (pb) | ISBN 9781315450322 (ebk)
Subjects: LCSH: World politics—21st century. | Political sociology. | Capitalism—Political aspects. | Elite (Social sciences)
Classification: LCC D863.3 .C678 2018 | DDC 327.1—dc23
LC record available at https://lccn.loc.gov/2018011341

ISBN: 978-1-138-21256-5 (hbk)
ISBN: 978-1-138-21257-2 (pbk)
ISBN: 978-1-315-45032-2 (ebk)

Typeset in Caslon
by Swales & Willis Ltd, Exeter, Devon, UK

Printed and bound in Great Britain by
TJ International Ltd, Padstow, Cornwall

This book is about the ephemerality of American, and by extension Western, civilization and is dedicated to all my students (1966–2016) from whom I learned a lot—and to the sea, which in the end vanquishes all powers.

* * *

> Thy shores are empires, changed in all save thee—
> Assyria, Greece, Rome, Carthage, what are they?
> Thy waters washed them power while they were free
> And many a tyrant since, their shores obey
> The stranger, slave, or savage; their decay
> Has dried up realms to deserts: —not so thou,
> Unchangeable save to they wild waves' play—
> Time writes no wrinkle on thine azure brow—
> Such as creation's dawn beheld, thou rollest now.
> —Lord Byron, *Childe Harold's Pilgrimage, Canto IV*

Contents

Acknowledgements		VIII
Preface		IX
Chapter 1	We Have a Problem	1
Chapter 2	Running Amok, or the End of Capitalism as We Know It	22
Chapter 3	The Failure of Alternatives	36
Chapter 4	The New Ancien Régime	50
Chapter 5	The Mindless Mind, or the New Wiles of Propaganda	70
Chapter 6	Another Rubicon? Reflections on Defeasance in the West	81
Chapter 7	Behemoth Lite National-Populist Democracy and Its Impact on Strategy	97
Chapter 8	When Nobody Minds the Shop	117
Chapter 9	Geostrategic Rivalries in a Period of Potential Deglobalization	128
Epilogue		140
Postscript After Pax Americana: Ten Theses on Geopolitical Disarray		142
Index		145

Acknowledgements

I wish to express my gratitude to many friends and colleagues: to Paolo Bruni, Carina Perelli, Anna Maria Jaguaribe, Volker Meja, Juan Rial, Christina Spellman, and Juan Carlos Torre for advice and ideas; to my wife Christina for her forbearance, to my colleagues in the Sociology Department at NYU for their tolerance of my courses out of the mainstream, and to Senior Editor Dean Birkenkamp for his encouragement of the project. Lorna Owen and Sarah Millward went over the manuscript with acumen and grace. Their support was invaluable; the shortcomings are solely mine.

Preface

To introduce this book and its topic, I must introduce myself and my reasons for writing it.

I have studied comparative social and political development during my 45-year career as a sociologist, which started as an undergraduate disciple of Herbert Marcuse and later as a graduate student assistant to Barrington Moore, Jr., at Brandeis University and Harvard University, respectively. I focused primarily on the social development leading to dictatorship and democracy in South America, and then branched out more widely to study the social bases and the political dynamics of fear-mongering regimes and authoritarian systems.[1] Subsequently, I joined the ranks of "transitologists" concerned with a wave of democratization in the late twentieth century, and collaborated with researchers in Europe and Latin America—in particular, with my late friend and Russian sociologist Victor Zaslavsky at Memorial University in Newfoundland, Canada and at the Institute of Advanced Studies in Lucca, Italy. Some of the ideas in this book were honed in conversations and debates I had with him and another late friend, Paul Piccone, founder of the quarterly journal *Telos*. Also, throughout my career I have studied and taught classical and contemporary sociological theory. Over my last five years at the Sociology Department of New York University, I became a self-taught "expert" on matters of conflict and war, under the broad umbrella of geopolitics—an area largely neglected by mainstream sociology and in need of correction on that score. The available literature on the subject of contemporary geopolitics has been largely written for professional military and security personnel. It is sometimes either too technical and detailed for the layman or too superficial, intended for politicians and public persuasion. In both cases it is thin on social theory, historical perspective, and appropriate comparisons. There is very little for the undergraduate student or the incipient graduate scholar in the social sciences, or for a curious lay reader who has no inclination toward starting a career in politics or in the administration of national or international security but has an intelligent curiosity beyond the smattering of opinion found in the editorial pages of newspapers or the evening news.

In my view, geopolitics is not just a body of apercus, a handful of basic rules, and a number of contrasting opinions on the state of international relations; it is a dynamic and ongoing mental discipline with a social and technological history. And so I decided to write a book to fill out this middle ground, to help an informed citizen or smart student to understand how and why the field of international relations and global affairs is where it is. The aim is to prompt and to deploy the sociological imagination.

This book is meant as a primer on the new geopolitics, based on both my research and teaching at NYU over the past few years which resulted in some successful courses at the undergraduate and the graduate level—one on the Sociology of Conflict and War, and the other on Sociology and Geopolitics.

In my long life in America, I have been a researcher and an incurable theorist. This is a calling that is not favored in the land. At the end of my academic career, I began to understand the American disdain for intellectuals—so different from countries like Germany and France, and even from my own native Argentina. In the society and economy of my adopted country, the world is an immediate one—of cause and effect, of rumor and fact, of advantage and deprivation. Despite having devoted my life to the pursuit of knowledge (and to sailing as an avocation), I can have some sympathy for the state of society that has occasioned that disdain. From time to time, I have reread Tocqueville on democracy, and admired his insight on early American culture—a culture that in many ways persists today. With a few distinguished exceptions, most of my students, pressured by circumstance, looked at learning as if it were a means to an end; at truth as if it were only a thing to be used. Values served their interests, rather than the other way around. In this book, I seek to redress the over-emphasis on practicality by reminding readers that beyond self-interest there lay larger forces and principles at work. In the end, they determine the fate of individual lives and nations.[2]

As an opening salvo, I will use the much-quoted half of a famous poem by William Butler Yeats, *The Second Coming*:

> Turning and turning in the widening gyre
> The falcon cannot hear the falconer;
> Things fall apart; the centre cannot hold;
> Mere anarchy is loosed upon the world,
> The blood-dimmed tide is loosed, and everywhere
> The ceremony of innocence is drowned;
> The best lack all conviction, while the worst
> Are full of passionate intensity.[3]

It is possible to translate the poem—so pertinent as of this writing—into contemporary and historical comparative sociology.

The quoted section of the poem captures the demise of geostrategic balance since the end of the Cold War and the closure of undisputed American hegemony. This for what concerns international relations. But then I will attempt to tackle parallel phenomena at the level of social relations and institutions. In this book, I propose to connect both levels of analysis in terms of different altitudes: first the global view of international relations at 30,000 feet—the realm of geopolitics; and then a look at social relations in a global web of ever thicker and often conflictive networks on the ground—that is the domain of sociology proper.

Notes

1 The building blocks and the architecture of authoritarian regimes have evolved since then, so that today illiberalism hides behind sham democracy. There is a growing bibliography on illiberal democracies. For similarities and dissimilarities between Latin American authoritarian regimes in the

1970s and the United States in 2017, see Juan Corradi *et al.*, eds., *Fear at the Edge. State Terror and Resistance in Latin America* (Berkeley, CA: The University of California Press, 1992), and David Frum, "How to Build an Autocracy," *The Atlantic*, February 2017.

2 I strongly recommend to young readers of this little book another little book that bucks the tide of immediate practicality: Abraham Flexner, *The Usefulness of Useless Knowledge* (Princeton, NJ: Princeton University Press, 2017). The original essay by Flexner is from 1939, and is accompanied in this edition by another essay from Robbert Dijkgraaf, "The World of Tomorrow."

3 William Butler Yeats, *The Second Coming*, 1919, www.poetryfoundation.org/poems/43290/the-second-coming.

1
WE HAVE A PROBLEM

The globe today needs more than ever forms of world governance, and never before in our lives has such governance been in shorter supply. This paradox has deep roots, and it is inexorably tied to the fate of a single world economic system that is also subject to another paradox: it is both triumphant and on the edge of collapse as a result of its own glaring contradictions. The task of this book is to unpack these two paradoxes and then take a glimpse at possible futures.

To unravel the first paradox, I propose to take a look at the evolution of geopolitics since the end of the Second World War. Immediately after the Second World War, two forces held the world together. The first and foremost was the so-called "balance of terror," in which two superpowers with very different socio-economic and political systems were stalemated by fear of mutually assured destruction. The second force was the response of the West to the related challenge that communism posed. It led to a relatively disciplined capitalism, under the protective umbrella of global institutions, most of them designed by the United States.

In the post-Cold War era, the world was glued together by these big global systems and by the US hegemon as their architect of record. We are now in the post-post Cold War world where global leadership and the glue of big systems are *needed more than ever*—because the simultaneous accelerations in technology, globalization, and climate change are weakening states everywhere, spawning super-empowered angry people and creating vast zones of disorder. And yet, despite the need for leaders and glue, humanity has a hard time confronting common problems and steering a course toward a viable future. The (mis)management of climate change offers a good example of the difficulty.

Climate Change: The Difficult Path toward Planetary Sovereignty

States or markets? That is often the question. In the ideological debates in the West, these two concepts are often treated as opposites. Conservatives argue that states interfere with the proper functioning of markets, that they slow growth, and that they distort the proper functioning of the economy. On the opposite side, left-leaning persons focus on market failures and on the noxious externalities that markets produce. And yet, on the one hand, it is hard to imagine well-run states that do not leave ample room for well-run markets or that do not abide by market signals. On the other hand, it is hard to imagine markets that do not rest on institutional frameworks that states have historically provided. Without some form of regulation and correction, markets are prone to run amok and crash. In short, states and markets are always combined. It is not simply that the truth lies somewhere in the middle—*in medias res*. The point is to find the proper synergy between states and markets. The question is whether their collaboration is mutually beneficial or dysfunctional, positive or perverse. The proper role of the state in the economy is different for different industries, countries, and periods. Getting it right is a matter of pragmatics, not ideology. I shall illustrate the point by quick reference to healthcare in America, and then move on to discuss the role of states and markets in managing climate change.

The endless pathologies of the American healthcare system illustrate, at a national level (on which I shall not dwell here), a perverse interaction between state and market. Government policies allow a medical-industrial complex to up-end any sane relation between cost and benefit. In a recent analysis of the complex, Elisabeth Rosenthal lists ten "economic rules of the dysfunctional medical market."[1] They can be summed up in one: "Prices will rise to whatever the market will bear"—which is much greater than what a well-functioning market should bear. With the help of a government captured by special interests, the American healthcare system functions like a protection racket with extortionate prices. Those who benefit from the racket are powerful enough to use government to protect their privilege. In every other advanced country, the government provides coverage to all citizens and provides a strong pushback to those who seek to use their market power to raise prices or to make money off unnecessary but lucrative treatments. In short, the market functions well when the state imposes discipline.

At the global level, nothing illustrates this better than the challenge that climate change presents—especially the impact of fossil fuel emissions on an increasingly crowded planet. In this respect, the world faces two types of geopolitical impasse. One is poor state capacity and the other is poor market capacity. I shall examine them in sequence.

Whatever one thinks of the benefits or disadvantages of the state upon the behavior of its people, it is an incontrovertible fact that the power of states has been weakened in an increasingly interdependent world. No government today can afford to ignore how "the markets" respond to its policies. No single state is powerful enough to tame global economic forces. When markets fail or have deleterious effects on human welfare, single states are impotent to mitigate such effects, let alone reverse a dangerous course. Only a super-state above all singular states could do that, and that super-state is absent. For the lack of something better, we have conferences, forums, treatises, multilateral organizations, and, alas, the United Nations. None of these goes much beyond a debating society. When it comes to the deterioration of the environment and of the human habitat, the knee-jerk reaction seems to be "everyone for him/herself and nature against all."

The international agreement on global warming, signed in Paris in December 2015 by 195 nations,[2] was a first step taken by the entirety of humanity in preventing and mitigating the disastrous effects of economic and population growth on the environment. Facing the intrinsic difficulties of collective action for the common good, the agreement was aimed at developing awareness in public opinion and building a new solidary subjectivity.

Twenty-three hundred years ago, Aristotle observed, "For that which is common to the greatest number has the least care bestowed upon it. Everyone thinks chiefly of his own, hardly at all of the common interest."[3] Aristotle's was the first formulation on record of what, in the twentieth century, came to be known as "the tragedy of the commons" (to be discussed below).

The Paris agreement is designed to decrease and mitigate the harmful impact of human activity on the planet's weather. In a nutshell, the objective is to reduce the warming of the Earth's atmosphere that could threaten life—not only human, but also the life of all other species as well—and degrade the environment in an irreversible way. For a graphic presentation of the environmental dilemma, I recommend a short lecture by the late statistician Hans Rosling, cited elsewhere in this book.[4] His argument boils down to this: as the world's population is projected to increase until it reaches ten billion at the end of this century (and then probably stop its growth as the birth and death rates equilibrate), billions of hitherto poorer people in the third world will reach a level of development once enjoyed only by the rich West (the biggest emitter of carbon dioxide). The latter—by then only 10 percent of the world's population—will have to adapt, reduce its own emissions, and share them more equitably with ten times as many people. Life would not be sustainable otherwise.

The representatives that signed the agreement celebrated it as a key milestone in history. They praised the diplomats' expertise in avoiding tensions and confrontations among diverse national interests, and thus, reaching an agreement considered satisfactory by everyone involved. In turn, the critics of the agreement—who shared the desire of stopping the planet's environmental degradation—contended that it was just a mere expression of principles and that, as with other good intentions, the signatories had just paved the way to hell. "Principles are fine," Napoleon is alleged to have said, but added, "They don't commit us to anything."

Upon examining the terms and clauses of the Paris agreement in their substantive merits, it is fair to say that it is neither too much nor too little. If the terms of the agreement went into effect as they are, in the best scenario the rhythm at which humanity dances toward disaster would slow down. Much depends on knowing how the weather works— an issue upon which too much uncertainty prevails. But it also depends on what can happen in the near future. Is it about the beginning of a revolution of the energy system we live by as well as the public policies that support it? Or rather, is it about a paper agreement that promises more than it is able to produce? It all depends on the actions that the different national and multinational leaderships will take. And this is the biggest risk. Many leaders are not interested in the global commons as a fragile treasure to bequeath to future generations, but as a bunch of resources to be exploited in a profitable way by groups upon which the leaders' support depend. National-populists are even willing to change the rhetoric from official piety to undisguised contempt for preservation, investigative reporting, and peer-reviewed science.

It is hard to unite humanity in a common approach to uncertain risks in a future that, to our short lives, might seem distant. It is something like drawing up a will in favor of our heirs' heirs. However, 195 countries did it. There is more: they committed themselves to act individually and jointly to reach consensual and measurable goals. Rich countries committed to financially and technically help poorer ones. And all of them—rich and poor—pledged to keep the increase in world temperature below 2 degrees centigrade.

So far so good, but let's examine the shortcomings. The Paris agreement is neither a treaty nor a contract. It is more an aspiration than an obligation underwritten by a transfer of funds and protected by actionable sanctions. For example, there are no limits on the emission of gases from vessels and aircraft. There is no mechanism to establish an international price for coal. Countries only promise to keep one another informed of their actions and keep their plans transparent. It is something like peer reviews in any scientific discipline, where papers circulate among experts. In the event of non-compliance or fraud, there is no other sanction than moral disapproval. Even worse, in the unlikely event that everybody involved strictly complies with the agreement, global warming cannot be restrained below the 2 degree centigrade rule.

Given these severe limitations, is it worth taking the Paris accord seriously? To answer this question, try to imagine the 195 participant countries as if they formed an academic department in a prestigious university. They are subject to the same dilemmas of collective action.

Each signing country must examine its plans and submit them to the peer review. Monitoring and transparency of those plans will be much greater than what exist today. Emergent countries with larger emissions (China and India) will be incorporated into this system. We could call this a model of "monitored aspirations." Even more important, everybody agrees to produce a reduction of emissions. None of the signatories can say that he or she is not interested in meeting the targets. With one lamentable exception: under a Republican government, the United States could easily and brazenly claim to be exempted from such review and thus torpedo the agreement. In such a case, the rest of the world, led by China, might tell them that after fifty years of considering themselves *primus inter pares*, the United States can ill afford to boast of superiority. The only result the Americans could obtain with this attitude is that their friends no longer trust them and their enemies no longer fear them.

Now let us assume the role of the devil's advocate with practical and theoretical arguments that will fuel doubts and skepticism. Among the practical arguments, we could say that despite twenty-five years of international negotiations regarding the weather, both the carbon dioxide emissions and the accumulated carbon stock in the atmosphere—as well as the per capita emission—have increased dangerously. If preventive actions had been taken in the early 1990s the current challenge would not be as serious as it is today. Although it is true that the carbon emission by productive unit (example: a super modern plant with low emissions) has decreased in the last years, the total economic growth in the world has unfortunately nullified the incidence of those individual improvements. The net result is negative. This brings us to a conclusion that runs counter to the assumption of economic science and of the business world: "growth at all costs." That assumption becomes less and less sustainable.

What Is to Be Done?

The Latin word *trivium* means the place "where three roads meet." In Roman towns, crossroads were congested with a lot of people. What today seems like an impasse may be no more than the dilemma we face in front of such a trivium.

To solve the impasse, there are three routes. Unlike the classic trivium, they are not dispersive. The first is via the formulation of emergency plans; the second, through massive investments in alternative and innovative technology. There is a third, through the development of economic models with a very different definition of "growth" from the one that prevails today.

Elinor Ostrom, the Nobel-prize winner in economics in 2009, represents an unorthodox school of economic thought. In a report on the governance of the commons, she makes clear that, within certain social groups, it is possible that cooperation and collective responsibility prevail over the exploitation of natural resources. There are groups that have developed mechanisms and institutions that do not follow either the logic of the private sector or the logic of the state.[5] Unfortunately, this is a minority position with only marginal examples to support it.

At the global level, the solution would be akin to creating some sort of "Apollo program" in relation to weather—like the United States once did to reach the moon. Such a project would involve two things: a great technological effort and an attainable consensus on what we may call "planetary sovereignty."

I will not dwell on the technological effort in this essay—but I hope for decisive changes at the frenzied pace of the ongoing technological innovations (an issue about which there is a large and positive bibliography). Instead, I will focus on the other mechanism: that of the collective action and attainable consensus, on which there have been several theoretical models in the social sciences.

The social trap or paradox of this collective agreement can be summarized in the words of the social theorist and commentator Barry Schwartz:

> How does one escape the dilemma in which multiple individuals acting in their own rational self-interest can ultimately destroy a shared limited resource—even when it is clear it serves no one in the long run? (...) We are now dealing with a tragedy of the global commons. There is one Earth, one atmosphere, one source of water and six million people are sharing it. Badly. The wealthy are overgrazing, and the poor can't wait to join them.[6]

What is true for individuals is also true for countries; when each individual acts in pursuit of his or her own interest, every interest gets ruined collectively. In 1968, the theoretician Garrett Hardin made this modern formulation of the old theories—from Aristotle's to Thomas Hobbes's.[7] Since then, every analyst who focuses on human action has not found a satisfactory solution *within the homo oeconomicus framework* of rational choice. For this reason, and since Hobbes, political theory has been forced to search for a solution *outside that framework* and name an actor above the individuals that can impose its diverse motives in the name of a superior and collective rationality. This actor traditionally was the state. According to this reasoning, when individual action leads to a crisis—generally an unresolved conflict of all against all—only the authoritarian imposition "from above" will be able to end the impasse and cut the Gordian knot. He who exercises this decision is sovereign; and the exercise of this "last resort" capability, accepted by every actor, is called sovereignty.[8] In this view, liberty is sacrificed to authority.

Until recently, sovereignty was the exclusive prerogative of nation-states and was recognized by international law. But in an era of intense and extensive globalization, common problems to every state have overwhelmed each one's ability to solve them, and have diminished their sovereignty. At the international level, the "tragedy of the commons" is fully in force. A global government or a super-state could overcome it. This remains only a remote possibility in the distant future. In the absence of such Leviathan maneuvers, a planetary sovereignty—only one or two superpowers—exercising the monopoly or oligopoly of decisional power and acting as a *de facto* global police force could stabilize the situation. But such arrangement belongs to the past and will not return. This was the "solution" to the dilemma applied during the Cold War and in the short term after the end of that bipolar geopolitics, with the surviving supremacy of the United States. Now, we are inside a full multi-polar reconfiguration of the world, with a clear decrease in sovereignty, both national *and* supranational. That is a serious impasse.

Experience shows that a group of nations without a central government overseeing them is incapable of solving crises in hard times. In a different book and in regard to Europe, I have tried to show how that impasse was reached.[9] As of this writing, European governments are realizing that the risk of European disintegration is real and more imminent than they thought possible. As a result, strategists in different European capitals are revising the assumptions regarding the inevitability of EU integration and the permanence of a military alliance with the United States. Some policy makers and independent analyses go further. They conclude that the EU, in its present form, is not likely to survive the 2021–2022 electoral cycles. The report by one consultancy states quite bluntly, "By the 2021–22 electoral cycle, the EU might be entering the last five years of its 'real' existence."[10]

Sometimes a serious external threat leads to the consolidation of a central power. Such is the case of a war against an identifiable and declared enemy with intentions of attacking. But there are other dangers and challenges that lead to a serious crisis without producing a solitary and "Hobbesian" reaction. In this case, the "enemy" presents itself in a catastrophic and dramatic way when it is too late.

In the face of such an impasse—and staying within the framework of mainstream economic science—other proposals have been put forward, some from unexpected quarters. For example, in the United States, some orthodox economists and Republican grandees have proposed a carbon tax.[11] The logic is fairly simple and it purports to reconcile individual incentives with a public good, the market with the commons. According to this proposal, a carbon tax can be revenue neutral—meaning that authorities impose a carbon tax on carbon-intensive goods and use that tax revenue, in turn, to reduce other taxes or to give people a carbon dividend. Since the dividend would be the same for everybody, there would be an incentive to emit as little as possible and enjoy the returns. In this sense, the carbon tax is socially progressive.

Despite denials from ideological zealots, scientists tell us that carbon released into the atmosphere has adverse effects on the climate. That is a classic example of a negative externality—a side effect associated with a certain form of economic activity. What some economists want to do is to internalize the externality. In other words, they want people to pay for the adverse side effects of their actions. A champion of liberty like John Stuart Mill, following his principle of "no harm,"[12] would agree with the following proposition: When your actions may harm somebody else, you pay for it, so you take that into account when you make your day-to-day decisions.

In America, some states are taking action independently of the federal government. An example is the state of Washington's Initiative 732, which proposes imposing a tax on carbon emissions. The revenue from the tax on carbon emissions would offset other taxes in the state—most notably, the sales tax and the business tax. The initiative has gained support from unlikely places, chief among them, Gregory Mankiw, a conservative economist and former head of George W. Bush's Council of Economic Advisers.

Regarding climate as well as other domains that affect the common fate of humanity, the larger question is: would it be possible to have an effective collective action in absence of planetary sovereignty? The drama of the so-called tragedy of the commons resides in the fact that the main enemy in this field is we humans—we have created an environmental Frankenstein.

The promissory novelty of the Paris climate accords is the origination of mechanisms and protocols of collective awareness, with the consequent delegitimization of a purely national collective conscience. We cannot move out of bad globalization by taking a step backwards, as is proclaimed by the frenzied and thoughtless nationalism that today pullulates each time there is a severe crisis. Facing the weather challenge, there is no more room for the slogan, "Our country first." We need another one more attuned to the situation: "Our common house (as the Pope says) or death."[13] The options, perhaps, are not so dire as this dichotomy suggests. *The options of the past* are what are obsolete. We are under pressure to search for new options vis-à-vis the new scenarios that unfold before our very eyes. The devil's advocate has convincing arguments but has not won the match yet.

To recapitulate, the argument about the first paradox with which we started: in the second half of the twentieth century, two massive systems competed for supremacy—liberal capitalism and state socialism. Today both have decayed, and in the face of such decay, diverse political movements are searching alternatives in an even more distant past. Alas, going back to the first part of the twentieth century is not only a fool's errand; it is extremely dangerous as well. So far, the only antidote is an emerging and collective awareness of severe risk.

*

This book seeks to unravel a second paradox, namely the terminal contradictions of the extant economic model that has prevailed since the end of the Cold War. To do so, I shall first examine the exhaustion of *each* of the contending systems that ruled humanity after the Second World War. I will provide tentative answers to two questions.

First, why did state socialism fail? In answering this we enjoy the benefit of hindsight. After all, the system is closed, and we can see the reasons for its demise—without, however, falling into the fallacy of *post hoc ergo propter hoc*.

The second question is a harder one to answer: in the words of Wolfgang Streeck, how will capitalism end?[14] To prepare the ground for an answer, I shall examine the political symptoms that are manifested in the decay of neo-liberalism—symptoms that sometimes parade as "solutions" when, in fact, there aren't any. One of the symptoms that parades as a solution is the revival of nationalism. A relapse into national-populism will not lead to an exit from the strategic impasse in the second decade of this century, or in any foreseeable future. It is, at best, a palliative measure for a deeper disease: behind the bombast (the alleged return to past grandeur), populist movements of the nationalist-kind evince mere delusions of adequacy.

In the search for more satisfactory answers, the final section of the book will provide a peek at bolder vistas of reform and reconstruction that might either prevent or follow the collapse of globalization, as we know it. A word of caution should be applied to that final section: we must avoid prediction but encourage readiness in the face of surprising events.

On Strategy and Predictability

A young journalist once asked Harold McMillan the following question, "Sir Harold, what do you fear most as Prime Minister?"[15] His answer was, "Events, dear boy, events."[16] In geopolitics, we should not dismiss facts that could seem inconsequent but that carry a long sequel of positive and negative consequences. We must acknowledge the importance of disproportion.

In the month of September, seafarers from the region where I sail (41° 29'24"N/71° 18'47"W) are on the lookout for the formation of tropical storms on the west coast of Africa, which by joining other forces, can rapidly transform into violent hurricanes that reach the Caribbean and move along the American coast up to Canada where they dissipate.

Meteorology has not advanced sufficiently enough as to make precise predictions regarding the intensity and trajectory of those destructive storms. Computers offer some probabilistic models, but these colossal storms always surprise us.

The reason for this unpredictability is the following: if, in a weather system, a small initial disturbance takes place, through an amplification of atmospheric conditions, it could generate a considerably big effect in the short or medium term. Example: a "tropical depression" or "wave" on the east coast of Africa can provoke major destruction in New York City. That happened with Hurricane Sandy, and more recently with Hurricane Harvey in Houston, Texas.

Today we can create a mathematical model of such dynamic and its effects. Without going over arcane formulas, the idea is as follows: given some initial conditions in a chaotic, dynamic system (specifically with sensitive dependence on initial conditions), any small discrepancy between two situations with a small variation in the initial data can result in trends where both systems evolve in completely different ways.

This is an old idea. It is called the "butterfly effect" in Chaos Theory. The name comes from variations of an ancient Chinese proverb: "The gentle flapping of a butterfly's wings can be felt across the world," or "a butterfly's flapping wings can cause a Tsunami at the other side of the world" as well as "the simple flutter of a butterfly can change the world." Go figure. The Chinese did.

It is also said that, in the old city of Syracuse, Archimedes argued, "Give me a lever long enough and a fulcrum on which to place it, and I shall move the world." The idea of a lever is the first formulation of the disproportionate effects of an action. These effects, perfectly calculable in Archimedes's physics, occur in real and short time. To estimate the disproportionate effects in long-time sequences from small variations in the initial data, we had to wait for the formulation of Chaos Theory—but even this cannot offer a practical guide to avoiding disasters.

What does all this have to do with geopolitics? Geopolitics deals with power relationships between countries and regions, but also *within* countries and regions.[17] In the past, geopolitics was the exclusive turf of statecraft. The field is much more complex now.[18] All sorts of actors are engaged in strategic calculations that do not stop at borders. Even when they are not making calculations, their actions often have strategic implications. Among these actors, there are those that are big and those that are small, the central and the marginal, the independent and the dependent, state organizations and non-state actors, including lone individuals. Sometimes their relationships and the resulting effects, throughout time and under different circumstances, surprise us; hence, the power of Sir Harold's "events." Also, in this field there are disproportionate effects in due course from variations in the initial data of a historic process, i.e., from actions and decisions that at the beginning seem insignificant or of contrary sign to that of later results. A clarifying example of this type of reasoning, regarding the alternative consequences of an historic event, was given a hundred years ago by the great sociologist Max Weber.[19]

Weber wondered whether a course of events, under analysis, would have stayed unaltered or would have been different from what is known. To illustrate this dilemma, the sociologist offered an example taken from ancient history that the historian Eduard Meyer had produced. In the battle of Marathon (490 BCE), the Greeks overcame the Persians. Based on the available knowledge, the larger understanding of the ultimate significance of this event requires presenting the objective possibility of how the actions could have developed if the Persians had won. The weight given to the importance of the Greek triumph is based on the fact that, had things turned otherwise, there would have prevailed a theocracy in Greece—as it happened in the other places where the Persians were victorious. The Greeks' triumph in the battle of Marathon thus became critical for the survival of the values of Western culture. This battle in a small corner of the Hellenic world had disproportionate and momentous effects for the destiny of the civilizations that followed, from Rome to today's Western world.

Postdiction has the immense advantage of hindsight; prediction is much more difficult. All a strategist can do is formulate plausible scenarios and be ready for a more or less adequate response to "events." In the art of seamanship (which I know better than the art of statecraft), the key term is *preparedness*; this entails two other aspects: *fitness* (material and intellectual) and *agency* (practice). The nations that stumbled into Word War I thought they were prepared. In retrospect they had no idea of the catastrophe that would befall them.[20]

The First World War began with a terrorist act in Sarajevo: the assassination of Archduke Ferdinand. Had the archduke's murderer failed in his attempt—and, even having succeeded—the great powers could have avoided the subsequent conflict. Sometimes, a mere contingency produces effects that, in the long run, seem pre-destined. *Post hoc ergo propter hoc.* The statement is a fallacy: we tend to project necessity upon contingency.

The butterfly effect functions not only in the destinies of entire peoples, but also in our own biographies. What would have become of my life if there had been no US scholarship in 1962, or if I had fallen sick on the day I was required to accept it? What would have happened to Argentine history if there had been no assembly of neighbors on May 25th, 1810 (the event that launched the South American wars of independence from Spain), or no massive rally on October 17th, 1945 (which brought Juan Domingo Perón to power)?

History is full of such examples of events that did not seem particularly significant in the moment but were crucial in the long run. The reverse is also true: there are events that seem momentous at the time of their occurrence but leave no lasting traces. The problem is that we generally do not realize the import of an occurrence except in retrospect. There is no clairvoyance at dawn, just wisdom at sunset. As Hegel said, "the owl of Minerva [the symbol of wisdom] spreads its wings only after dusk." However, certain awareness that there are many butterflies flapping their wings helps us to design better strategies through a map of possible alternatives.[21] No strategy is foolproof, but a proper strategic vision is aware of the possible scenarios.

In our era of globalization, one thing is certain: time and space have been thoroughly compressed. The trope "far away and long ago" is no longer valid. For our argument, this means not only that there is the occasional "butterfly flapping," but also that flappings are multiple, simultaneous, and cross-linked. Our civilization has achieved making what was previously complicated easier—but at a cost: complexity increases and predictability diminishes. "Complicated" and "complex" are not the same conditions. Today, it is much simpler to communicate at long distance, but much harder to know where the communication networks, collectively and individually, are leading us.[22]

Sometimes, the arts and literature anticipate worlds that take years for the social sciences to discover. Jorge Luis Borges captured the complexity of globalization as early as 1943 in a short story, which bears the name of the first letter in the Hebrew alphabet, the Aleph. In the tale, Carlos, a hack poet, tells the narrator that his house is threatened by demolition and explains that he must keep the house because the cellar contains an Aleph, a mysterious object that helps him write a poem he has been working on with dogged determination. Though the narrator believes Carlos to be quite insane, he proposes, without waiting for an answer, to come to the house and see the Aleph for himself. Left alone in the darkness of the cellar, the narrator begins to fear that the poet is conspiring to kill him, and then he sees the Aleph:

> On the back part of the step, toward the right, I saw a small iridescent sphere of almost unbearable brilliance. At first I thought it was revolving; then I realized that this movement was an illusion created by the dizzying world it bounded. The Aleph's diameter was probably little more than an inch, but all space was there, actual and undiminished. Each thing (a mirror's face, let us say) was an infinite thing, since I distinctly saw it from every angle of the universe. I saw the teeming sea; I saw daybreak and nightfall; I saw the multitudes of America; I saw a silvery cobweb in the center of a black pyramid; I saw a splintered labyrinth (it was London); I saw, close up, unending eyes watching themselves in me as in a mirror; I saw all the mirrors on earth and none of them reflected me; I saw in a backyard of Soler Street the same tiles that thirty years before I'd seen in the entrance of a house in Fray Bentos; I saw bunches of grapes, snow, tobacco, lodes of metal, steam; I saw convex equatorial deserts and each one of their grains of sand.[23]

Complexity defies prediction. In contemporary "risk society,"[24] it is difficult to see a crisis coming and even more difficult to trace its origins, which are frequently anodyne. At the same time, we do not know if that crisis merges with others similar in character. In meteorology, the convergence of separate disturbances can produce a "weather bomb" or perfect storm.

Europe today is an example. In recent years, a lot has been written on the European geopolitical situation. The key to this European predicament can be summarized as follows: to the demographic crisis (an ageing and declining population in Northern Europe facing a demographic bulge in the Middle East), add the political crisis (democracy and legitimacy deficits), a monetary crisis, the fiscal crisis of the European periphery (the bankruptcy of Greece), the greater assertiveness of Russia, and last, the humanitarian crisis of refugees from Northern Africa. These are crises of different—even remote—origins, diversely dynamic, with long-term advantages and benefits that are hard to discern, but that converge in time and space at a speed that overwhelms the decision-making capacity of a weak and doubtful leadership.

Regarding the First World War and its seemingly trivial origin in the Balkans, Churchill crafted the famous phrase for those small and unstable countries: "They produce more history than they can consume."[25] Today, that phrase applies not only to small countries on the periphery but to all countries. It is hard to know with certainty which events are eventful.

But let us not despair. Sometimes humanity owes a big favor to someone who has produced more history than he or she was capable of consuming. Examples abound. The Marathon warriors, quite inferior in number to their enemies, stopped the development of the Persian civilization. The small country of Vietnam, over various decades, managed to curtail the imperial arrogance of great powers; it defeated China, France, and the United States. The small island of Cuba curtailed American imperial arrogance for half a century. The small and land-locked country of Switzerland became the world's banker. We should not ignore the dangers of disproportion, but neither should we dismiss the occasional benefits.

In any event, preparedness, as described earlier, is essential for coping in a world of great complexity and disproportion. It is the *sine qua non* of a proper strategic vision. By proper strategic vision, I mean the following: a flexible realpolitik (close attention to facts and a consideration of possible factual scenarios) guided by transcendent values that do not stop at national borders. As for these values, if "universal" sounds over-ambitious—and it has been over-used—different countries could settle for a set of values that can gather around them a *cosmopolitan consensus*.

Given the deficiencies of both national and international institutions as presently constituted, only well-informed publics around the world can forge a cosmopolitan consensus. Yet, at the ground level of daily life things are as complex as they are at the conventional heights of geopolitics. In the era of social media, distraction is the bane of our much-touted connectedness. To clarify this argument, I will bring to bear a perhaps unexpected parallel from theology.

In his *Confessions*, Saint Augustine took stock of his own career in light of his conversion to Christianity and came to a special characterization of sin in the interpretation of his newly acquired faith. In his view, at the root of the old catalog of deadly sins (derived from the Jewish tradition)—such as concupiscence, gluttony, vanity, and so forth—as well as at the heart of less truculent secular habits or activities (many of them considered respectable and even commendable), he saw a terrible waste of time and energy in the pursuit of worldly goals, to the detriment of spiritual perfection and of a focus on salvation. Augustine considered the essence of sin to be in seeking to find one's ultimate pleasure in the things that God has made as opposed to in God Himself. "My sin was this: That I looked for beauty, pleasure and truth, not in Him, but in myself and in His other creatures."[26] In short, for Augustine the root of all sins was distraction.

The tension between immanence and transcendence, between worldly activity and otherworldly concerns is a constant in all major religions. Within Christianity, the Protestant ethic was an attempt at reconciling the dichotomy by sanctifying practicality as a form of spiritual discipline. The well-known thesis of Max Weber still holds. The reformed religiosity-sponsored productivity was as a manifestation of preordained righteousness and shunned satisfaction, whether immanent or transcendent. It was a pure *terminus a quo*, not a *terminus ad quem*.

But the fetishism of method could not solve the Augustinian tension and was always haunted by its own success and the ensuing temptation of good results.[27] The problem of distraction reappeared with a vengeance—in economic parlance as clarifier of theology, sin became a threatening externality.

Today, both in the conflicts within and between political systems and in the business of daily life, Augustinian distraction prevails as never before. Distraction from what? In secular terms, it is distraction from an economy and a society that serve human flourishing. In the Pope's words, only new communal organizations can liberate people from the bondage of "individualism and the despondency it spawns."[28] Mindless activism and spurious "productivity" distract us from the ecology of the surrounding world and ruin the commons. This kind of busyness—enhanced by social media—functions like a narcotic. New opiates—real and metaphoric—have become the pseudo-religion of the people.

Notes

1 Elisabeth Rosenthal, *An American Sickness: How Healthcare Became Big Business and How You Can Take It Back* (New York: Penguin Press, 2017), 8.

2 Bill Chappell, "Nearly 200 Nations Adopt Climate Agreement at COP21 Talks in Paris," NPR, December 12, 2015, www.npr.org/sections/thetwo-way/2015/12/12/459464621/final-draft-of-world-climate-agreement-goes-to-a-vote-in-paris-saturday.

3 Aristotle, *Politics, Book 2*, section 1261b, trans. Benjamin Jovett (London: Batoche, 1999).

4 "Population Growth and Climate Change Explained by Hans Rosling," YouTube video, 3:18, posted by *The Guardian*, on May 20, 2013, www.youtube.com/watch?v=SxbprYyjyyU.

5 Elinor Ostrom, *Governing the Commons: The Evolution of Institutions for Collective Action* (Cambridge, UK: Cambridge University Press, 1990). More recently see Elinor Ostrom *et al.*, *The Future of the Commons. Beyond Market Failure and Government Regulation* (London: Institute of Economic Affairs/IEA, 2012).

6 Barry Schwartz, "Tyranny for the Commons Man," *The National Interest*, July/August 2009, http://nationalinterest.org/print/article/tyranny-for-the-commons-man-3153.

7 His article was originally published as "The Tragedy of the Commons," *Science*, 162 (1968): 1243–1248.

8 See Carl Schmitt, *Political Theology: Four Chapters on the Concept of Sovereignty*, trans. George Schwab, with a foreword by Tracy B. Strong (Chicago, IL: University of Chicago Press, 2004).
9 Juan E. Corradi, *Why Europe? The Avatars of a Fraught Project*, 2013, Amazon e-Book, www.amazon.com/s/ref=nb_sb_noss?url=search-alias%3Dstripbooks&field-keywords=Juan+Corradi++Why+Europe%3F&rh=n%3A283 155%2Ck%3AJuan+Corradi++Why+Europe%3F.
10 Rosa Brunello and Lucio Caracciolo, "Europe in the Brexit and Trump Era: Disintegration and Regrouping," MacroGeo, February 27, 2017, www.macrogeo.global/nexus/europe-in-the-brexit-and-trump-era-dis-integration/.
11 Jerry Taylor, "The Conservative Case for a Carbon Tax," Nikanen Center, March 23, 2015, www.hks.harvard.edu/hepg/Papers/2015/Taylor%20 Conservative%20Case%20for%20a%20Carbon%20Tax.pdf.
12 John Stuart Mill, *On Liberty* (London: Longman, Roberts and Green, 1869), www.bartleby.com/130/.
13 On Pope Francis's cosmopolitan populism, see Austen Ivereigh, "Is the Pope the Anti-Trump?" *The New York Times Sunday Review*, March 5, 2017.
14 Wolfgang Streeck, *How Will Capitalism End? Essays on a Failing System* (London and New York: Verso, 2016).
15 Harold McMillan was Prime Minister of the United Kingdom from January 10, 1957 to October 19, 1963.
16 The quote has been much discussed and much critiqued: www.telegraph.co.uk/comment/personal-view/3577416/As-Macmillan-never-said-thats-enough-quotations.html.
17 For a concise discussion of the concept, see Klaus Dodd, *Geopolitics. A Very Short Introduction*, Chapter 1 (New York: Oxford University Press, 2014).
18 Pierre Bourdieu, "The Field of Cultural Production, or: The Economic World Reversed," *Poetics*, 12 (November 1983): 311–356. I use the term "field" in Pierre Bourdieu's sense of a dynamic area of conflict around a specific set of issues in which actors vie for status and forceful dominance.
19 Max Weber, "Objective Possibility and Adequate Causation in Historical Explanation," *The Methodology of the Social Sciences* (Glencoe, IL: Free Press, 1949), 173–174.
20 See Max Hastings, *Catastrophe 1914. Europe Goes to War* (New York: Alfred A. Knopf, 2013).
21 Pierre Bourdieu called this *le champ des possibles* (the field of the possible).
22 See Nicholas Carr, *The Shallows: What the Internet is Doing to our Brains* (New York: W.W. Norton, 2011).

23 Jorge Luis Borges, *The Aleph and Other Stories*, trans. Andrew Hurley (2000, repr., New York: Penguin, 2004).
24 Ulrich Beck coined the term in *The Risk Society. Towards a New Modernity* (New York: Sage Publications, 1992).
25 Winston Churchill, http://world.time.com/2012/10/08/the-balkan-wars-100-years-later-a-history-of-violence/.
26 www.shmoop.com/augustine-confessions/sin-quotes.html.
27 As well presented by Daniel Bell in *The Cultural Contradictions of Capitalism* (New York: Basic Books, 1978).
28 Ivereigh, "Is the Pope the Anti-Trump?"

References

Aristotle. *Politics, Book 2*, section 1261b, trans. Benjamin Jovett. London: Batoche, 1999.

Augustine. *The Confessions*, www.shmoop.com/augustine-confessions/sin-quotes.html.

Beck, Ulrich. *The Risk Society. Towards a New Modernity* (New York: Sage Publications, 1992).

Bell, Daniel. *The Cultural Contradictions of Capitalism* (New York: Basic Books, 1978).

Borges, Jorge Luis. *The Aleph and Other Stories*, trans. Andrew Hurley (2000, repr., New York: Penguin, 2004).

Bourdieu, Pierre. "The Field of Cultural Production, or: The Economic World Reversed," *Poetics*, 12 (November 1983): 311–356.

Brunello, Rosa and Lucio Caracciolo. "Europe in the Brexit and Trump Era: Disintegration and Regrouping," *MacroGeo*, February 27, 2017, www.macrogeo.global/nexus/europe-in-the-brexit-and-trump-era-dis-integration/.

Carr, Nicholas. *The Shallows: What the Internet is Doing to our Brains* (New York: W.W. Norton, 2011).

Chappell, Bill. "Nearly 200 Nations Adopt Climate Agreement at COP21 Talks in Paris," *NPR*, December 12, 2015, www.npr.org/sections/thetwo-way/2015/12/12/459464621/final-draft-of-world-climate-agreement-goes-to-a-vote-in-paris-saturday.

Churchill, Winston. http://world.time.com/2012/10/08/the-balkan-wars-100-years-later-a-history-of-violence/.

Corradi, Juan E. *Why Europe? The Avatars of a Fraught Project*, 2013, Amazon e-Book, www.amazon.com/s/ref=nb_sb_noss?url=search-alias%3Dstripbooks&field-keywords=Juan+Corradi++Why+Europe%3F&rh=n%3A283155%2Ck%3AJuan+Corradi++Why+Europe%3F.

Dodd, Klaus. *Geopolitics. A Very Short Introduction*, Chapter 1 (New York: Oxford University Press, 2014).
Hastings, Max. *Catastrophe 1914. Europe Goes to War* (New York: Alfred A. Knopf, 2013).
Ivereigh, Austen. "Is the Pope the Anti-Trump?" *The New York Times Sunday Review*, March 5, 2017.
Mill, John Stuart. *On Liberty* (London: Longman, Roberts and Green, 1869), www.bartleby.com/130/.
Ostrom, Elinor *et al*. *Governing the Commons: The Evolution of Institutions for Collective Action* (Cambridge, UK: Cambridge University Press, 1990).
Ostrom, Elinor. *The Future of the Commons. Beyond Market Failure and Government Regulation* (London: Institute of Economic Affairs/IEA, 2012).
"Population Growth and Climate Change Explained by Hans Rosling," YouTube video, 3:18, posted by *The Guardian*, on May 20, 2013, www.youtube.com/watch?v=SxbprYyjyyU.
Rosenthal, Elisabeth. *An American Sickness: How Healthcare Became Big Business and How You Can Take It Back* (New York: Penguin Press, 2017).
Schmitt, Carl. *Political Theology: Four Chapters on the Concept of Sovereignty*, trans. George Schwab, with a foreword by Tracy B. Strong (Chicago, IL: University of Chicago Press, 2004).
Schwartz, Barry. "The Tragedy of the Commons," *Science*, 162(3859) (1968): 1243–1248.
Schwartz, Barry. "Tyranny for the Commons Man," *The National Interest*, July/August 2009, http://nationalinterest.org/print/article/tyranny-for-the-commons-man-3153.
Streeck, Wolfgang. *How Will Capitalism End? Essays on a Failing System* (London and New York: Verso, 2016).
Taylor, Jerry. "The Conservative Case for a Carbon Tax," *Nikanen Center*, March 23, 2015, www.hks.harvard.edu/hepg/Papers/2015/Taylor%20Conservative%20Case%20for%20a%20Carbon%20Tax.pdf.
Weber, Max. "Objective Possibility and Adequate Causation in Historical Explanation," *The Methodology of the Social Sciences* (Glencoe, IL: Free Press, 1949), 173–174.

2
Running Amok, or the End of Capitalism as We Know It

The purpose of this chapter is twofold. The first objective is to understand the increasing difficulties of capitalism in managing its internal contradictions in a global environment. The second objective is to understand the social and political processes triggered by such difficulties. In turn, these two tasks will serve as a prelude to comprehend the geopolitical disarray that has resulted from internal distractions in the major powers (and amplified by strategic errors) and in particular to explain the relative decline in the geopolitical stance of the United States.

Although the economics of capitalism is never steady state, during the three decades that followed the Second World War, the advanced capitalist societies of the West experienced remarkable social and political stability—as opposed to the fitful societies in the periphery. Dynamic capitalism could coexist with stable societies. In such societies most of the population accepted the basic features of the status quo. Authority was sufficiently diffused so that there was no single set of levers of command powerful enough to move the entire society in one direction. Both revolution and reaction seemed to be things of the past. Those three decades—known in Europe as *les trente glorieuses*—were characterized by prosperity, steady upward mobility, a social sense of security, and a political compromise between the major parties, perhaps best exemplified by the American bipartisan consensus on internal peace and external strategy. The basic consensus arose out of multiple individual and sectorial interchanges. Under such conditions, the parties that sought power combined a large variety of claims to create a broad political base. Different pressure groups with pet projects and pet grievances had to discuss their differences, and no single group showed a vocation to change society as a whole, or to upset the entire apple cart. Parties competed over large clienteles and made myriad tactical alliances. A famous maverick of tactical alliances was President Lyndon B. Johnson, but Republican President Ronald Reagan and Democratic Speaker of the House Tip O'Neil extended the practice beyond the *trente glorieuses* with an *entente cordiale*. With variations, similar ententes prevailed in other Western nations, including a power-sharing arrangement between Italy's long-ruling Christian Democrats (at the national level) and the Italian Communist Party (at the local level).

Things have changed dramatically since the period of prosperity and stability. The most serious changes have occurred on two levels: the global and the local. At the global level, capitalism has reached systemic completion (it is explained below in this chapter). At the various local levels, globalization has produced severe social dislocation, and this in turn generates growing resentment against the system as a whole (it is described in the chapters that follow).

In the past, capitalism always had a future. It does not seem to have one any longer. It has become an unstoppable force as it accumulates profits, propels inequality and insecurity to hitherto unsurpassed levels, and damages life. In the end the mad rush will stop and the train will crash, leaving a trail of devastation. When Roman civilization—based on a different mode of expansion—finally collapsed, it left among the wreckage seeds of future rebirth. It also left solid architectural structures—which make magnificent ruins, as illustrated in Piranesi's etchings. If and when late capitalist civilization and its epitome—the American way of life—collapse, they may leave only toxic consequences to a stunned and over-crowded humankind. There will be no aqueducts to admire, only plastic water bottles to lament.

The world of business can illustrate the troubling trend. In a clearly thought-out argument, Simon Head, a Senior Fellow at both Oxford and New York University, outlines the strategies and mechanisms through which capitalist bosses, empowered with scientific management and IT systems, have created a world of top-down control where workers are de-skilled, de-moralized, and very insecure in their precarious existence. In the United States, where these developments have reached grotesque proportions, the blame is quite often, and now officially, placed on the outside. To put it in the standard vulgate, other countries—especially the developing ones—"steal" American jobs. But blaming others merely masks the basic driving force, to wit the relentless pursuit of profit not only by outsourcing production, but also, at the very heart of what stays at home, through specific management systems.

> There now exist in the US economy of the new century these very powerful agents of industrialization, known as Computer Business Systems (CBSs), that bring the disciplines of industrialism to an economic space that extends far beyond the factories and construction sites of the industrial economy of the machine age: to wholesale and retail, financial services, secondary and higher education, health care, 'customer relations management' and 'human resource management (HRM),' public administration, corporate management at all levels save the highest, and even the fighting of America's wars.[1]

The resulting paradox is this: in alienating human abilities and debilitating resistance, in overcoming union blowback, and in depressing the wages of an insecure working class—in short, in creating a vast reserve army of the supernumerary, late capitalism undermines the economy itself. The money is there; the jobs are not. In late capitalism, when 20 percent of the population owns 80 percent of the stock, we cannot assume that that system can increase growth. It wallows in a swamp of unmanageable surpluses—surplus capital on one end, surplus people on the other. Financialization and concentration are such that there are only so many mansions, super yachts, fast cars, and fancy watches the wealthy can buy. From his grave in Highgate, Karl Marx may well say, "I told you so," except this time the proletariat is bypassed. That class is being rapidly replaced by an ex-proletariat in now defunct industrial sites,[2] and by a post-proletariat—also known as the precariat[3]—in what used to be the middle class. Little wonder then that the new social constellation has upended political loyalties.

The evolution of critical social theory reflects the paradox of late capitalism. The loss of old alternatives and the failure of socialism have led some oppositional intellectuals to an almost desperate search for genuine (as opposed to artificial) "negativity" and thus to an encounter with odd bedfellows.

A theoretical journal, with which I was once associated, illustrates the intellectual paradox:

> In the past decade and a half, the journal *Telos* has attained a certain level of notoriety for having engaged in a not unsympathetic debate with some of the leading figures of the European New Right, for tarrying with an extremely conservative form of populism which pits decentralized, so-called "organic" communities against the monolithic power of the New Managerial Class that resulted from the New Deal, and for advocating a brand of federalism not unlike that of the clearly xenophobic Italian *Liga Norda* and for rehabilitating the political theory of Carl Schmitt who was instrumental in drafting the Nazi Nuremburg Laws. In themselves, such positioning would be controversial enough; however, this is especially true in the case of a journal that has played an unrivalled role not only introducing critical theory, and to a lesser extent, French post-structuralism to a North American audience, but also in seeking, on this basis, to provide a sustained analysis and critique of American society.[4]

The confusion of intellectuals is a mirror of the confusion of everybody else.

In pursuit of my line of thought we may well ask, what took this contradiction so long to reach an explosive point? The answer to this question is within reach.

In the past, capitalism went through many cycles of boom and bust, short and long, and experienced crises large and small. Through all of them, capitalism managed to survive, reaching ever-new heights of development. It was a remarkable achievement, based in part on this:

capitalism always had a non-capitalist outside that either capitalism could colonize or that could resist it and through such resistance forced it to reform. This last point merits attention.

Resistance stimulates self-discipline. It prolongs the life of a system that otherwise has a tendency to commit suicide. In 1990, Georgi Arbatov, then director of the Institute for the Study of the USA and Canada in the tottering Soviet Union, told American visitors to Moscow, "We are going to do a terrible thing to you—we are going to deprive you of an enemy."[5] With the benefit of hindsight, we can say he had a point.

When confronting an enemy that was powerful in both material and ideological ways, and that controlled many states and the terms of political debate in large parts of the world, the dominant system in the West (liberal capitalism) was disciplined by the combination of its ambition and the need to face the challenge. Inside its own society, the established system's primary task was twofold: to deliver the goods, and to maintain and win believers. That task forced the West to cajole and confront, to engage and rival the "other" internally and externally. As it succeeded in this hegemonic competition, it confidently accepted a temporary compromise with some of the objectives of the enemy and with softer allies that otherwise could bolt. This was the price of power, but it was also an insurance policy against its own contradictions. The system thus developed suppleness, buoyancy that enabled it to either avoid or survive serious crises, and to gain adherence beyond its core base.

When the system lost these challenges, it became ensconced and habituated to uncontested power. Its leaders and representatives got out of previous practice.[6] They lost touch with external reality, and thus dimmed their strategic vision. Actually, after the Cold War, both the Clinton and the Bush administrations in the United States thought they could "create" geopolitical reality and mold facts to their will. Such smug self-assurance was also evident among the leaders of the European Union. The impulsion to understand challenges and to anticipate difficulties disappeared. The system dominated the entire geopolitical field for a while but, paradoxically, grew isolated and doctrinaire. Arguments it once had to sweat through against serious opponents became lazy nostrums or worse, spectacularly wrong, as with the proclamation of "the end of history"—a Hegel-lite thesis for sophomores.

None other than Friedrich Hayek, the patron saint of conservatives, predicted the possible demise of capitalism. The free-market ideal, he said, would become stationary when it is most influential. In a similar vein, Joseph Schumpeter argued that Marx had been right about the non-viability of capitalism in the long term, but for the wrong reason. It wasn't class conflict that would bring about the transition to some other system, rather the processes of concentrating technology and capitalism that would cause its own end, either with a bang or with a whimper.

Whether automation has the effect of reducing profits through the elimination of human labor as a source of profits (as predicted by Marx in the first draft of his *magnus opus*[7]) or through shrinking the pool of consumers, the overall outcome is likely to be roughly similar. If we follow Schumpeter's reasoning—without a need for productive workers, and confronting the concentration of purchasing power in ever-smaller circles—the days of free-market capitalism seem numbered. The British historian Lord Acton was right in stating "absolute power corrupts absolutely." As the hold of the system on supple management slips, and the impulse for artificial negativity (a concessionary strategy) wanes,[8] so does its hold on public legitimacy.

Success can be the road to ultimate failure. To make my argument terse: late capitalism has lost the constraint of circumstance to stop it from eating itself. Remember the shout of Polyphemos after Odysseus and his crew blinded him in order to get out of the cave in which he had imprisoned them: when his fellow Cyclops asked who was it that had wounded him, the monster answered with the name that the wily Greek hero had given him, "Nobody." The challenges are there and they will be legion, but the system's vision is blurred and the reaction—though brutal—will be, I am afraid, very clumsy. To put things in perspective, let me quote a classic source, this time from ancient Rome:

> ...when the commonwealth had grown through hard work and justice [...] and wild nations and mighty peoples subdued by force, and Carthage—the rival of Rome for command of an empire—had been eradicated, and all seas and lands became accessible, then Fortune began to turn savage and to confound

everything. Those who had easily tolerated hard work, danger and uncertain and rough conditions, regarded leisure and riches [...] as a burden and a source of misery. Hence it was the desire for money first of all, and then for empire, which grew; and those factors were the kindling (so to speak) of every wickedness.[9]

Under the present global dispensation, capitalism seems both unstoppable and autonomous. It may very well be at the end of its historical accomplishment. I sometimes use the archaic word "compleat" to refer to this late stage in capitalist development. It is an earlier spelling of "complete," sometimes used phrasally in allusion to manuals or compendiums like one of my favorite books, *The Compleat Cruiser: The Art, Practice and Enjoyment of Boating* by L. Francis Herreshoff. The term contains a double entendre: it alludes both to success and to finitude, to achievement and termination.

Those "in the cockpit" can enjoy its privileges but do not seem capable of steering or repairing it. The system is prone to a self-destructive acceleration. In this scenario, large sectors of the population are faced with the dilemma of trying to join, merge with it, even somehow cling to the edges, or step out of its way. But if they step out, or are left behind, what is there for them to do?

Meanwhile, and always in this scenario, inside the system, there are signs of an aging process, as the term "late capitalism" suggests. We should beware of facile biological analogies, but the following seems apt to me. Within the last decade, a new theory of aging has gained acceptance among biologists. As theoretical physicist Michio Kaku indicates,

> Basically, aging is the buildup of errors, at the genetic and cellular level. As cells get older, errors begin to build up in their DNA and cellular debris also starts to accumulate, which makes cells sluggish. As cells begin to slowly malfunction, skin begins to sag, bones become frail, hair falls out, and our immune system deteriorates. Eventually, we die.[10]

Of course, cells have self-correcting mechanisms (in economic systems; an example from the past is Keynesian policies, and from the present "quantitative easing"). "Over time, however, even these error-correcting mechanisms begin to fail, and aging accelerates."[11]

To write about the end of capitalism would seem like engaging in speculative fiction. Obituaries of it were legion since its early days, and all of them were premature. And yet, it is an unavoidable exercise when we realize that all systems and institutions have a beginning and they also have an end. However, there is a perverse twist to a simple diagnosis of historical obsolescence: sometimes what vanished in the past seems to return in a different avatar. For instance in our disorganized world, human trafficking has emerged as a real scourge, suggesting that slavery has reappeared in a slightly different guise. Defeasance on one level may provoke the resurgence of what had been repressed. What we are watching today is not a homeostatic return to the system's health but instead a return of pathologies that so many thought had long been left behind: dictatorship, nationalism, xenophobia, and zealotry are but a few of the old demons released anew.

In its present stage, advanced or late capitalism is characterized by a steady decline in its rate of growth—even in those countries like China that have seen decades of sustained and quite spectacular development. Not only is Chinese growth slowing down, but is beset by rising debt as its government piles up mountains of financial obligations. In the United States and Europe, debt is a heavy burden on citizens and governments alike. In the periphery, debt crises are common and extreme, often leading to a collapse of entire economies, or their survival in a state of suspended animation, where each bailout is used to pay the interest on older debt—a veritable Ponzi scheme of multilateral "support."

Debt is a bet on the eventual resurgence of growth, but it may not be a good bet. Acquiring debt can be an expression of confidence on a future based on solid prospects. Or it can be a mechanism of avoidance of what one is afraid to encounter. Debt is Janus-faced. In Roman mythology, Janus was the god that presided over passages, gates, and endings—doors that opened on pleasing vistas or fateful ends. Life or death, smile or tears. One of Janus's faces was hope; the other one was fear. We are in full transition. Janus presides.

As a sharp rise of inequality accompanies slow growth and bigger debts, distributional conflicts multiply. There are more claimants for a share of a pie that is not commensurate to their expectations. Slow growth, debt, and inequality reinforce each other and form a vicious circle that seems out of control. The very legitimacy of a system based on the promise of material betterment begins to wobble when the benefits fail to reach those without capital. Under explosive occurrences, like the financial meltdown of 2008, the discourse of mainstream economics failed to encompass important dimensions of the crisis, and even the specific economic emergency took economists by surprise. There is a need for the analysis of the entire social structure. However, the hour of need finds a discipline like sociology, which should supply a more encompassing diagnosis, devoid of the proper analytic tools. It has long abdicated its former interest in political economy. Methodological virtuosity and the proliferation of subfields do not add up to a vision of the whole.

As a preliminary exercise in the sociological imagination, I submit that late capitalism is caught in a double contingency: on the one hand TINA (There Is No Alternative), and on the other hand a serious, if not terminal, IC (Internal Contradiction). Scylla and Charybdis. Is there a way out? I will anticipate my answer, and then supply the sociological arguments for it. The answer is: yes and no. Yes, because it is rationally conceivable. No, because there is no collective agent, no social Odysseus to lead through the exit path.

Toward a Good Society?

Many years ago, Herbert Marcuse—who was my teacher and who had become, despite himself, a guru of the New Left—gave a lecture on liberation at the time of the Vietnam War. During the Q&A period that followed, an angry middle-aged businessman challenged him to present a blueprint for a good society. Faithful to Hegelian negativity, Marcuse answered, "A good society is a society without business." Surely the philosopher had doubled down on the provocation, but to my mind, his answer went beyond a sarcastic riposte or a mere boutade.

Marcuse—an old critical Berliner marooned in Massachusetts and later California—meant that it was not the task of business to manage, at the current stage of civilization, the basic necessities of life, to wit: health, education, and welfare. Advanced industrial society could easily provide the fundamental needs of humankind, the negative *freedoms from*—disease, hunger, destitution, and ignorance—and do so without charge. Beyond the realm of necessity managed by non-capitalist and collective institutions, lies the realm of positive *freedoms to*—create, explore, compete, invent, and yes, a robust freedom of enterprise. This interpretation of Marcuse's terse answer stayed with me for many years.[12]

It occurred to me that the standard ideologies of radical change at the time of my youth envisioned a state of (relative) bliss beyond the lure and rigor of the market. In short, the good life was expected to come *after* capitalism. In fact, the opposite is true: the basic good life should come *before*. Needs satisfied in a collective manner as public goods should be the platform, the ground, and the threshold of free enterprise. Only beyond need stands the promise of a fuller life, of conscious risk-taking, of excellence in sport, of daring imaginings, including quests for wealth and competitive achievement.

Looked at this way, contemporary society seems to have put the cart before the horse. With its alleged magical allure, the market has invaded the commons, colonized the life world, substituted wants for needs, and turned public (indivisible) goods into private (divisible) goods. As a result, human life—even in prosperous countries—has become very insecure. Risk has shifted from the public to the private, from the collective to an individual left to his or her own devices that are soon found to be insufficient.[13] The social dysfunctions of the shift are visible today in the widespread antinomian and resentful individualism that is the other side of the globalist coin.[14]

The cart, however, was not always placed before the horse. In their developmental process, the most dynamic and successful economies of the world today were far from free markets at their takeoff stage.[15] The time is ripe to re-enact this dialectic of market and non-market—and reverse their directional movement at the stage of mature, even late, development—under penalty of collapse.

We don't have to go far in search of the basic principles of change. The first and foremost is the expansion of universal protection not just for infants, the aged, and the truly desperate, but also for everybody. Today only a few privileged persons are able to lead meaningful lives in spite of the worries about health, bankruptcy, loss of job, cost of education, old age, and the outside world that prevail in the heartland of dynamic capitalism: America. How can our physical, intellectual, and economic well-being be insured against the risks of modern life and its fragile ecology?

Various schemes to secure the world of work can be and should be rationally discussed—ranging from wage insurance to retraining vouchers to basic and universal income. In the same vein, a universal single-payer system of health insurance has to be examined calmly and in an informed manner. Similarly, guaranteed affordable access to all levels of education should be considered a necessity, not a luxury in the struggle for existence. One of the most ambitious but commonsensical policy proposals is from Professor Jacob Hacker that advocates for a universal insurance program that "would protect workers and their families against catastrophic drops in their incomes and budget-busting expenses."[16] I will not dwell on the details of his or other proposals but simply refer to the impressive conclusion of his book, which I consider a primer on doable, practical reforms that could save late capitalism from itself.

Here, I will emphasize something more general—namely the rather urgent need for a return to universals at a moment in which the reaction against an imbalanced globalism is leading angry people and opportunistic leaders, *urbi et orbi*, to embrace particularism as an illusory safe haven. At the level of civil society, this illusory refuge takes many forms: racism, xenophobia, identity politics, competitive victimology, monadic and tribal withdrawal—all under the veil of connectivity and liquid interaction. At the level of countries as whole units, the illusory refuge takes the form of chauvinism and national security. But neither the towers of Babel nor the battlefields of civil or interstate wars are solutions for humanity's problems. Alas, such irrational, particularistic, and counter-productive actions are, for the moment, likely to prevail. Recalling an ancient myth, these are the siren songs in the strait of

Messina that lure sailors to perdition. Hence, the stratagem of Odysseus to secure safe passage through the straits. It worked but only temporarily as six men died, and then the entire ship was wrecked—and in the end, only Homer's hero survived. But the question for sociology, not mythology, is another one. Has the erosion of collective agency under late capitalism gone so far that neither institutions nor social movements can push for the necessary and radical reforms? If a good society is "a society without business," how do we reconcile such desideratum with the better-known (and popular) expression, "the business of America is business?" Only if we take care of basic needs through other than pure market means. Moreover, "business" comes in different forms and styles-—some very good and some quite noxious, as the literature on the variety of capitalisms shows. Such calibration is beyond the capacity and the understanding of vast sectors of the voting population in most real or nominal democracies today.[17] What if the good society is a society that nobody wants?

Notes

1 Simon Head, *Mindless. Why Smarter Machines are Making Dumber Humans* (New York: Basic Books, 2014), 3; also, http://policyoptions.irpp.org/magazines/old-politics-new-politics/head/.
2 See Nicholas Eberstadt, *Men Without Work: America's Invisible Crisis* (West Conshohocken, PA: Templeton Press, 2016).
3 The term was coined by Guy Standing in *The Precariat: The New Dangerous Class* (London: Bloomsbury Group, 2016).
4 Gary Genosko, Samir Gandesha, and Kristina Marcellus, "A Crucible of Critical Interdisciplinarity: The Toronto *Telos* Group," *TOPIA* 8, 2002, https://topia.journals.yorku.ca/index.php/topia/article/viewFile/153/144.
5 Arnold Beichman, December 29, 1990, www.beichman.com/Articles/ARBATOV.htm.
6 I will not claim originality for this insight. Many theorists in the past foresaw that possibility. The proposition goes as far back as the Roman historian Sallust, who maintained that unchallenged success undermined Roman society and culture. As Mary Beard wrote "In Sallust's view, the moral fibre of Roman culture had been destroyed by the city's success and by the wealth, greed and lust for power that had followed its conquest of the Mediterranean and the crushing of all its serious rivals." Mary Beard,

S.P.Q.R. A History of Ancient Rome (New York: Liveright Publishing Corporation, 2915), 38. I supply the original quote below.
7 See Karl Marx, *Foundations of the Critique of Political Economy*, trans. Martin Nicolaus (1973, repr., New York: Penguin, 1993). Written 1851–1861, published for the first time in 1939 by the Marx-Engels Institute, Moscow.
8 For the original thesis of artificial negativity, see Tim Luke, "Culture and Politics in the Age of Artificial Negativity," *Telos*, 35 (March 20, 1978): 56–72.
9 Sallust, *Catiline's War, The Jugurthine War, Histories* (London: Penguin, 2007), 8.
10 Michio Kaku, *The Future of the Mind* (New York: Doubleday, 2014), 281.
11 Kaku, 282.
12 As a student of socio-economic development, I rapidly realized that "really existing" socialism was in fact a propaedeutic project to catch up with established capitalism. Later, in the shift from Mao to Deng in China, the hypothesis seemed confirmed. The problem is that, once attained, capitalism in China has acquired the same dis-orientation as capitalism in the West.
13 See Jacob S. Hacker, *The Great Risk Shift: The New Economic Insecurity and the Decline of the American Dream* (New York: Oxford University Press, 2008).
14 Perhaps in an exaggerated way, such is the argument of Pankaj Mishra, *Age of Anger: A History of the Present* (New York: Farrar, Straus and Giroux, 2017). See also David Goodhart, *The Road to Somewhere. The Populist Revolt and the Future of Politics* (London: Hurst and Company, 2017).
15 As argued by Ha-Joon Chang, *23 Things They Don't Tell You About Capitalism* (New York: Bloomsbury Press, 2011), 62–73.
16 Hacker, *The Great Risk Shift*, 191.
17 American geo-strategists like George Kennan and Zbigniew Brzezinski have long lamented the negative propensity of the American public toward needed rational reform of the system from which it has so greatly benefitted. "We have a large public that is very ignorant about public affairs and very susceptible to simplistic slogans by candidates who appear out of nowhere, have no track record, but mouth appealing slogans"—www.goodreads.com/author/quotes/123814.Zbigniew_Brzezi_ski. See also Zbigniew Brzezinski, *The Grand Chessboard* (New York: Basic Books, 1997). For his part, Kennan saw in America a land consumed by "unrestrained decadence," so much so that in his diaries he considered himself a guest in his culture, not a member of the household. George F. Kennan, *The Kennan Diaries* (New York: W.W. Norton, 2014).

References

Beard, Mary. *S.P.Q.R. A History of Ancient Rome* (New York: Liveright Publishing Corporation, 2015).

Beichman, Arnold. December 29, 1990, www.beichman.com/Articles/ARBATOV.htm.

Brzezinski, Zbigniew. *The Grand Chessboard* (New York: Basic Books, 1997).

Chang, Ha-Joon. *23 Things They Don't Tell You About Capitalism* (New York: Bloomsbury Press, 2011).

Eberstadt, Nicholas. *Men Without Work: America's Invisible Crisis* (West Conshohocken, PA: Templeton Press, 2016).

Genosko, Gary, Samir Gandesha and Kristina Marcellus. "A Crucible of Critical Interdisciplinarity: The Toronto *Telos* Group," *TOPIA* 8, 2002, https://topia.journals.yorku.ca/index.php/topia/article/viewFile/153/144.

Goodhart, David. *The Road to Somewhere. The Populist Revolt and the Future of Politics* (London: Hurst and Company, 2017).

Hacker, Jacob S. *The Great Risk Shift: The New Economic Insecurity and the Decline of the American Dream* (New York: Oxford University Press, 2008).

Head, Simon. *Mindless. Why Smarter Machines are Making Dumber Humans* (New York: Basic Books, 2014).

Kaku, Michio. *The Future of the Mind* (New York: Doubleday, 2014).

Kennan, George F. *The Kennan Diaries* (New York: W.W. Norton, 2014).

Luke, Tim. "Culture and Politics in the Age of Artificial Negativity," *Telos*, 35 (March 20, 1978): 56–72.

Marx, Karl. *Foundations of the Critique of Political Economy*, trans. Martin Nicolaus (1973, repr., New York: Penguin, 1993).

Mishra, Pankaj. *Age of Anger: A History of the Present* (New York: Farrar, Straus and Giroux, 2017).

Sallust. *Catiline's War, The Jugurthine War, Histories* (London: Penguin, 3007).

Standing, Guy. *The Precariat: The New Dangerous Class* (London: Bloomsbury Group, 2016).

Streeck, Wolfgang. *How Will Capitalism End? Essays on a Failing System* (London and New York: Verso, 2016).

3
The Failure of Alternatives

A dark but stable period in geopolitics—the Cold War—has long passed. After a 20-year hiatus under the illusory hegemony of a single superpower, it seems that the peace dividend was squandered. As a result, the world should be engaged in catching up with the opportunities lost—*à la recherche du temps perdu*. But is it? Can the time lost be made up so that peace and prosperity follows, or will a number of decaying systems produce lamentable performances, secular stagnation, renewed tensions, chaotic international relations, and hot wars?

For a while there was a bit of hope that what remained of socialism and a new reformed capitalism could be reconciled. The re-establishment of Cuban—US relations reinforced that impression. Could this have been Pope Francis's first miracle? It is doubtful, since miracles are never reversed, and in the United States, as of this writing, the Trump administration is undoing all of Obama policies. However, during the Obama administration, the Pope had managed to induce a thaw in the glacial and hostile interdependency of Cuba and the United States. It was tantamount to turning the twilight of two systems into a dawn. American liberal capitalism and Cuban socialism had each seen better days. For a moment they seemed to move toward some sort of reconciliation.

Later on, however, America's aggressive retrenchment from internationalism and liberal democracy has changed the equation. It is too soon to discern a method in the seeming disarray that ensues, and the ultimate outcome. Facile predictions are to be avoided, but a reasoned analysis of alternative scenarios is more necessary than ever.

In other sections of this book, I examine the strategic impasses of American power in the twenty-first century. In this chapter I will tackle the legacy of the Cuban revolution in particular, and the impasses of socialism in general—including those of the left worldwide. While a requiem may be sung for various socialisms, we cannot discard the eventual resurgence of some of the historical tenets and positions of progressive forces that are today in retreat. On a small scale, Cuba is a microcosm that shows the dilemmas inherent in a socialist alternative and the strategic impasse to which they lead.

Ten years after the triumph of the Chinese revolution, Cuba underwent its own upheaval. The Cuban revolution provoked extraordinary interest throughout the world. In the middle of the Cold War, the country acquired a geopolitical significance out of proportion to its size and almost triggered a terminal nuclear exchange between the two superpowers. Under the Russian umbrella, Cuba projected influence and placed operatives, even troops, in the developing world. In those days, the Cuban defiance was not lost on the rest of Latin America or on what was then called the Third World. As in the stands at a baseball game, it took only a small country or a small group of countries (Vietnam immediately comes to mind) to start a wave.[1] Different from a baseball game, this wave was neither fun nor frivolous. To alarmed American officials and inspired Third-World revolutionaries alike, Cuba seemed capable of setting off a chain of transformative events.

The importance of Cuba, however, was of a different kind. The Cuban revolution was the latest of a series of socialist experiments moving beyond capitalism toward a new society of radical equality. The Cuban revolution vowed to "build a new man" and demanded nothing less than a new conception of human nature. The prestige of the revolution rested primarily on the equalization of social conditions and on universal access to health and education—two achievements attained with record speed during the first decade of the regime.

Those of us who were young in 1960 remember the passionate curiosity that the Cuban experiment sparked. In the West, postwar prosperity had given rise to libertarian hopes among the youth. In the communist

East, the Cuban revolution seemed also to offer an alternative to hidebound regimes.

From a sociological point of view however, we must pose two different questions: one, to what extent were those achievements linked to the totalitarian form of the regime that took shape during the initial surge of the revolution? Two, what price did Cuban society pay for the relentless pursuit of egalitarian inclusion? Is there an inner logic that connects the enforcement of social justice with the absence of civic and public rights, with police repression, and with the prohibition to move abroad?

There was an intimate association between two processes during the first decade of the revolution—namely, the rapid equalization of conditions that the revolutionary regime imposed on the entire society and the extraordinary concentration of power in the figure of Fidel Castro. The one made no sense without the other. The revolutionary project was to transform society from the top and from a high point of control. The project rode on a wave of popular enthusiasm and a collective feeling of emancipation from a corrupt and despotic past.

The revolution was not the replacement of one despotism for another, but something very different: a radical overhaul of existing inequalities that required central control *and* mass participation. The coincidence of the rational and the charismatic is a phase through which all revolutions pass. However, in the long run, rationality trumps passion, and charisma becomes bureaucratically routinized. The Cuban peculiarity consisted in the persistence of charisma and the longevity of Fidel. It provided the regime with long-range stability but ultimate fragility.

We must remember the speed, the depth, and the manner of construction of an egalitarian society during the first phase of the revolution: the rapid equalization of society from the bottom up, favoring the rise of the downtrodden and the excluded, but enforced "without ifs or buts" from the top of political power. Radical equalization and centralization of control were two sides of the same coin. It was not just an incidental oddity of the Cuban trajectory. The historical and comparative record shows that socialism has not been able to de-couple those two processes.

The first ten years witnessed two agrarian reforms: the first, an expropriation, break-up, and redistribution of large holdings to the landless; and the second, an imposition of state control over all agricultural production, large and small. The non-agrarian sectors of the economy too were nationalized: foreign subsidiaries, sugar refineries, commerce, utilities, and construction. The state also took control of health and education, and regulated housing. All these measures favored those at the bottom of society and progressively alienated those above—first the privileged elite and then the middle class. Each wave of equalization produced a corresponding wave of exile—initially the recalcitrant, then the disenchanted. It was a period of "terror and progress." Popular mobilization went hand in hand with severe repression.

At the top level of leadership, a voluntaristic model of forced development prevailed (embodied by Ernesto 'Che' Guevara and subsequently by Fidel Castro himself) with the stress on altruism as opposed to material incentives. In practical terms, the process eliminated all the economic agents that were not agents of the state.

What was the upshot? In the society, there was a radical leveling of distinction; in the economy, a phenomenal disorganization of production. The economic dislocation happened in part due to the exodus of qualified people, but more significantly due to the inability of the state to allocate activities without market signals. The former was a serious but temporary effect, the latter a fatal flaw.

The centralization of control in the hands of one person and the repression of any other center of decision-making affected not only the "natural" enemies of the revolution, for example landowners and businessmen, but its original supporters as well. The control and "coordination" of student organizations, of labor unions, and finally of the cultural and artistic producers have been well documented. A similar process occurred with the single party of the revolution, which through successive purges became a docile communist machine subordinated to Fidel. As in other Soviet-type regimes, those in the cockpit were in constant fear of falling out of favor.

For the wider society, quieter forms of "organized consensus" gradually replaced the initial enthusiasm of revolutionary mobilization.[2] A vast network of surveillance and thought control was established throughout the committees for the defense of the revolution, by police informants, and by the active encouragement of denunciations of neighbors, relatives and friends. Daily life passed from a state of cheer to a culture of fear. The result was the corrosion of civil forms of conviviality. From an economic point of view, it meant the downgrading of initiative and morale, which reinforced the incompetence of the state and required ever more unpleasant dispositions, like stock outs and rationing.[3]

If, on the political level, the regime survived through repression, on the macro-economic level, it was on the dole of the Soviet Union. When the latter collapsed, Cuba suffered enormous penury until it was partially bailed out by Hugo Chavez's oil-rich Venezuela. The aggressive and clumsy foreign policy of the United States helped to provide a justification for tightening control. But ultimately, the model of a Soviet-type society was the product of a deep internal logic.

Forced equality produced economic disincentives and dysfunctions that negatively affected growth and prosperity—among them ersatz full employment, absenteeism, theft of public property, a clandestine market, and a "double morality" of conformity and deviance at the same time. Moreover, the regime soon discovered that social inequality has not one source but many—and that the regime was generating its own.

As the original leadership faced old age, Cuba teetered unprepared for a transition to a world that, although mired in crises, no longer accepted the mode of life that Cubans had withstood during a heavy 50 years. Today, Cuba does not fare better on many comparative indicators than it did in 1959. Comparing it with poorer Caribbean nations will not do—the comparison is with Chile, Uruguay, or Brazil. Now, as then, the relative position is pretty much the same.

The conclusion is sobering: Cuba has attained greater social equality at the price of political repression and economic stagnation. It has lived in a bubble of silence and denial, a museum of a way of life that nobody wants. For more than 50 years, the revolution spent the moral capital it held as a bastion of dignified resistance to the colossus of the north. That is Cuba's sociological and geopolitical impasse.[4]

The question pending for the future is how to accede to a modality of economic growth that does not destroy the social achievements of the past—how to throw away the communist bathwater without ejecting the egalitarian baby as well. That is a tall order indeed.

In a critical assessment of Soviet ideology and morality in 1958, Herbert Marcuse expressed a cautious optimism about the potential of a socialist system to eventually transcend the perpetual struggle for existence inherent in capitalist society. He made two claims: (a) that in a fully nationalized economy, there are no inherent forces that would resist accelerated and extensive automation either on the part of management or on the part of labor, and (b) that the transfer of control from above to below would be relatively unproblematic and take place while retaining the same social base (nationalization).[5] These claims have been disproven by subsequent historical developments. If the potentiality ever existed, it became moot as the Soviet system collapsed. Instead, what superseded it was a somewhat grotesque caricature of Western mores: a voracious consumerism in the underlying population, and a conflation of capitalism and grand larceny at the top.

In the surviving Soviet-type societies like Cuba—as in the defunct Soviet Union—that reach the limit of their developmental potential, the power elite faces a conundrum: how to maintain legitimacy and stability without growth (the socialist version of "secular stagnation"[6]). As sociologist Victor Zaslavsky has shown, in those systems, consensus can be achieved neither through terror nor through the voluntary identification of social groups with regime goals, but only through the successful manipulation of conflicting latent group interests. Under these conditions, serious political-economic reforms are practically inevitable. Other alternatives, like a remilitarization of society through nationalist appeals, are too costly and could only postpone the reckoning of the elite with the internal contradictions of the system.[7] But advancing reforms may bring latent group conflicts into the open, and ultimately result in the collapse of the entire edifice of the state. For the socialist elites, the impasse is clear: damned if you do; damned if you don't.

The world does offer examples of managed transitions from egalitarian socialism to unequal but prosperous capitalism—some more attractive than others. In a few intellectual and policy circles, there is discussion of the "Vietnamese way" in which the communist power structure itself sponsors an opening of the country to capitalist investment, while protecting not just its own interests but also social solidarity. A superficial overview of social behavior however, raises the question of whether the Cubans—after decades of force-fed altruism—have lost their appetite for solidarity and the initiative for entrepreneurship that East Asians managed to retain.

If the Cuban leadership decided to undertake "Vietnamese reforms," the situation would look like this. The regime would propose measures that would give greater scope to the private sector, reduce the budget deficit, and boost the output of agricultural and consumer goods in order to raise market supplies and exports. Specifically, the government would seek to make prices more responsive to market forces and to allow farmers and industrial producers to earn profits. Barriers to trade would be lowered; the checkpoint inspection system that requires goods in transit to be frequently inspected would be abolished; and regulations on private inflow of money, goods, and tourists from overseas would be relaxed. In the state-controlled industrial sector, overstaffing in state administrative and service organizations would be slated for reduction. Government leaders would also plan to restructure the tax system to boost revenue and improve incentives. Non-traditional exports such as ethanol would increase, while outside investors would regain their faith. As in Vietnam, the economy would then grow at 6 percent or more a year, and inequality would increase (an inevitable byproduct of a capitalist surge), but poverty would diminish significantly. With luck and investments coming from another tropical republic—Brazil—Cuba could mitigate its dependence on foreign fossil fuels and become a net exporter of sugar ethanol. The transition for Cuba would be another large social experiment, this time based no longer on the socialist proposition that sacrifice should be shared equally, but on the capitalist proposition that a rising tide lifts all boats.

In the immediate future, Cuba will navigate treacherous waters—a passage full of danger between the reefs of two rent-seeking mafias, one inside the country and the other one outside: on the one hand, the attempt by exiles to settle accounts, and on the other, the pretensions of functionaries of the regime to become the new capitalist masters, Russian-style.

In 1953, a young rebellious student named Fidel Castro led a failed assault on the fortress of Moncada. He was arrested and tried. In defending himself, he gave a speech that became famous, "History will absolve me." For the next 60 years, history was kind to him because he controlled it. The other "History" to which he referred in his youthful speech could not possibly absolve him—because it does not exist. What remains of its ghost is a troubling question mark under which Fidel and his system withered dismally with age.

Given the historic failure of state socialism, what possible futures await us? Is the impasse of Cuban socialism a symptom of a more general malaise? Will the left ever get out of such dead ends as Cuba has encountered? What forces within capitalism itself will propel a re-examination of non-capitalist solutions to acute economic, social, and political problems both inside countries and in the global commons? First, I will examine the general implications of the Cuban case, and then—in a broad sketch—how the prospects of a terminal crisis in late capitalism may prompt key actors to experiment with alternatives.[8]

The Cuban example suggests a number of explanations of why socialism is today in disarray. One partial explanation has to do with historical fatigue, which I have described, and the extraordinary longevity of Fidel. Behind this particular fatigue lies a deeper cultural trend, namely the high price that has historically been paid for two basic socialist tenets: radical equality and collective solidarity.

For the masses worldwide, it would seem that individualism trumps collectivism as a preferred way of life, and yet evinces a strong current of dissatisfaction—what Sigmund Freud named "disquiet" or *Unbehagen*.[9] The advances in technology reinforce this trend.

We may well have moved into a territory that has little to do with either classic liberalism or classic socialism. We certainly have moved beyond individualism and its more regimented successors—as have been discussed in the well-known theses of David Riesman's *The Lonely Crowd*[10] and Philip Slater's *The Pursuit of Loneliness*.[11]

In his 2009 sociology guidebook to the new world of social relations,[12] Dalton Conley wrote that instead of individuals searching for authenticity, we are "intraviduals" defined by shifting personas and fast evolving electronics, which help us to manage "the myriad data streams, impulses, desires and even consciousnesses that we experience in our heads as we navigate multiple worlds." The humans of "Elsewhere Society," Conley argues, are only convinced they're in the right place, doing the right thing, at the right time, when they're on their way to the next destination. Constant motion is a balm to a culture in which the very notion of authenticity ... has been shattered into a thousand e-mails.

In another track of speculative sociology, *Liquid Love*, Zygmunt Bauman wrote of people who are "despairing of being abandoned to their own wits and feeling easily disposable," and as a result are "desperate 'to relate'"[13]—but can't really relate.

More recently, and better grounded in data, Sherry Turkle argues that smartphones and social media have crowded out real conversation.[14] Digital technology has led to an atrophying of human capacities like empathy and self-reflection. However, in the subjects she interviewed, Turkle detected a real yearning to reassert themselves and behave like adults—a finding that gave her a measure of hope.

Increased, faster communication and electronic connectivity have fragmented society, with the occasional exception of mass protests spurred by social media that go as easily as they come, and fail to transform society. These pop-up movements actually upend the traditional socialist pattern of political behavior—in which long organizational preparation preceded mobilization—with more lasting consequences. Recent research seems to confirm this diagnosis.[15]

Yet neither flash mobilization—sometimes massive but ephemeral— nor classic forms of socialist organization, which lead to centralized decision-making, provide solutions to the crisis-prone and disruptive nature of "late" (some would say moribund) capitalism.[16] The latter resembles a self-driven car liable to crash and hurt its passengers. In the current perverted form of this economic system, concentration and gross-wealth inequality (the capitalist equivalent of stultifying socialist central control) are not only de-moralizing and unfair, but they are also arguably the very roots of economic crises like the financial meltdown of 2008. It is in the wreckage left by such crises where one can sometimes glimpse the glimmer of a ghost of hope: the self-organization of local communities.

During Argentina's economic collapse (national default) of 2001– 2002, I observed in the city of Buenos Aires the spontaneous growth of grassroot initiatives in the neighborhoods of what had been, until then, a fairly smug middle class. Collective decision-making, participatory budgeting, and an orderly barter economy were the order of the day. I witnessed an astonishing phenomenon in that emergency: the appearance of "Soviets of the middle class."

A more standard form of state-sponsored normalization eventually overtook those emergency initiatives. But their mere appearance prompted my curiosity. Could people help grow such storm sprouts into sustainable forms of economic and social organization? Answers to this question are not mere exercises in utopian dreaming. Under the present system, many more—and worse—emergencies await us. The existing web of social relations cannot cope with the powerful thrusts of technological and production forces. Alternative forms of conviviality will be imperative for survival.

There is an active search for such alternatives, in theory and in practice, and not just by academic researchers or marginal retreatists. An example is a 2011 book by the former British diplomat Carne Ross.[17] He lists a few tested low-level economic experiments like worker-owned companies that merge the commercial with the democratic, resulting in a fair distribution of bonuses, and social and recreational facilities while maintaining profit as a valid pursuit. In the financial sector, and following the proposals of economist Laurence Kotklikoff,[18] Ross cites limited purpose banking (LPB) and mortgage mutual funds as institutional antidotes to high-risk and predatory lending. In these cases, contingent liabilities would be backed by capital. As for riskier trades, they would be allowed, provided that the assets of bankers and brokers are on the block in case of failure.[19] In the domain of health care, cooperatives more responsive to patients than to profit-oriented insurance companies would be the basis of a system that is a neither private nor public. In the sphere of production, cooperatives would manage profit-sharing schemes that are participatory, egalitarian, and yet perfectly compatible with the attractions of competitive capitalism.

These and other such experiments have one thing in common: the devolution of power to local communities, with taxes and revenues moving from central collection and distribution to the grassroots level where people are in control over budgets and policy. Together they could greatly reduce social inequality in interesting and non-repressive ways. Already in today's societies—with all their imperfections, economies with greater wealth equality enjoy better mental health, lower crime, and a sense of well being, according to the research of Richard Wilkinson and Kate Pritchett.

If and when late capitalism enters a death spiral, there will be a need for these grassroots, bottom-up social arrangements to pick up the pieces and inform a process not of reconstruction but of construction of a different, more sustainable, and satisfying civilization.

Notes

1 The study of behavioral dynamics shows that processes other than rational choice shape human action and can have historical significance. See Elias Canetti, *Crowds and Power*, trans. Carol Stewart (London: Victor Gollancz, 1962; New York: Farrar, Strauss and Giroux, 1984). Also Mark Earls, *Herd: How to Change Mass Behavior by Harnessing Our True Nature* (New York: Wiley, 2007).
2 On the concept of "organized consensus," see Victor Zaslavsky, *The Neo-Stalinist State* (Boston, MA: M.E. Sharpe, 1982). For a review of Zaslavsky's original insights on the structure and dynamics of soviet-type societies, see Veljko Vujačić, "Victor Zaslavsky's Contribution to the Study of Soviet-type Societies," *Ventunesimo Secolo*, 30 (February 2013): 193–204.
3 "The Disadvantages of Socialism," Boundless.com, www.boundless.com/business/textbooks/boundless-business-textbook/economics-and-business-2/businesses-under-socialist-systems-30/the-disadvantages-of-socialism-164-6530/. The Cuban experience seems to confirm the classic critique of socialism by Austrian school economists, such as Friedrich Hayek and Ludwig Von Mises, who argued that the elimination of private ownership of the means of production would inevitably create worse economic conditions for the general populace than those that would be found in market economies. Without the price signals of the market, they stated that it is impossible to calculate rationally how to allocate resources.
4 There seems to be an awareness of this impasse among members of the Cuban Communist Party. See for instance, Pedro Camp, "Cuba Needs a Participatory and Democratic Socialism," *Z Blogs* [blog], April 21, 2010, https://zcomm.org/zblogs/cuba-needs-a-participatory-and-democratic-socialism-by-pedro-campos/.

5 Herbert Marcuse, *Soviet Marxism: A Critical Analysis* (New York: Columbia University Press, 1958), 256–257.
6 Economist Alvin Hansen coined the phrase in a 1938 address to the American Economic Association. Harvard economist Larry Summers recently brought it back into the mainstream. "This is the essence of secular stagnation," Hansen explained, "sick recoveries which die in their infancy and depressions which feed on themselves and leave a hard and seemingly immovable core of unemployment." Alvin Hansen, "Economic Progress and Declining Population Growth," *The American Economic Review*, 29(1) (March 1939): 1–15.
7 War mobilization has been used by great powers as a solution to a deep and prolonged socio-economic impasse, with the world-shattering results that we all learned from two world wars. For smaller nations which try this path out of an internal stalemate, the results are not earth-shattering but are immediately catastrophic for the regime in power—as in the case of Greece in 1974 and Argentina in 1982.
8 See for instance, Wikipedia, s.v. "Predistribution," last modified December 12, 2016, https://en.wikipedia.org/wiki/Predistribution.
9 Sigmund Freud, *Civilization and Its Discontents*, trans. James Strachey (London: Hogarth Press and Institute of Psychoanalysis, 1930; New York: W.W. Norton, 2010).
10 David Riesman, *The Lonely Crowd: A Study in the Changing American Character* (New Haven, CT: Yale University Press, 1961).
11 Philip Slater, *The Pursuit of Loneliness: American Culture at the Breaking Point* (Boston, MA: Beacon Press, 1970).
12 Dalton Conway, *Elsewhere USA: How We Got from the Company Man, Family Dinners, and the Affluent Society to the Home Office, BlackBerry Moms, and Economic Anxiety* (New York: Pantheon Books, 2009), 21.
13 Zygmunt Bauman, *Liquid Love* (Cambridge, UK: Polity, 2000), www.smh.com.au/articles/2003/06/20/1055828481958.html.
14 Sherry Turkle, *Reclaiming Conversation: The Power of Talk in a Digital Age* (New York: Penguin, 2015).
15 See Zeynep Tufekci, "Does a Protest's Size Matter?" op-ed, *The New York Times*, January 27, 2017. Also see her book, *Twitter and Tear Gas: The Power and Fragility of Networked Protest* (New Haven, CT: Yale University Press, 2017).
16 My use of the term differs from the parsing of other scholars like Wolfgang Streeck, (Streeck, *How Will Capitalism End?*). The concept of late capitalism has been in circulation since the publication of Natalia Moszkowa, *Zur Dynamik des Spätkapitalismus* (Zurich: Verlag der Aufbruch, 1943). The

name has been in use among Marxists, critical theorists, and cultural commentators. In a very general sense, it denotes a stage in the development of the world economy dominated by the fluidities of financial capital.

17 Carne Ross, *The Leaderless Revolution: How Ordinary People Will Take Power and Change Politics in the 21st Century* (New York: Blue Rider Press, 2011).
18 See Laurence Kotklikoff, *Jimmy Stewart is Dead: Ending the World's Ongoing Financial Plague with Limited Purpose Banking* (New York: John Wiley and Sons, 2010).
19 William D. Cowan, "Welcome Back, Wall Street," *The New York Times*, February 12, 2017.

References

Bauman, Zygmunt. *Liquid Love* (Cambridge, UK: Polity, 2000).
Boundless.com, "The Disadvantages of Socialism," www.boundless.com/business/textbooks/boundless-business-textbook/economics-and-business-2/businesses-under-socialist-systems-30/the-disadvantages-of-socialism-164–6530/.
Camp, Pedro. "Cuba Needs a Participatory and Democratic Socialism," *Z Blogs* [blog], April 21, 2010, https://zcomm.org/zblogs/cuba-needs-a-participatory-and-democratic-socialism-by-pedro-campos/.
Canetti, Elias. *Crowds and Power*, trans. Carol Stewart (London: Victor Gollancz, 1962; New York: Farrar, Strauss and Giroux).
Conway, Dalton. *Elsewhere USA: How We Got from the Company Man, Family Dinners, and the Affluent Society to the Home Office, BlackBerry Moms, and Economic Anxiety* (New York: Pantheon Books, 2009).
Cowan, William D. "Welcome Back, Wall Street," *The New York Times*, February 12, 2017.
Earls, Mark. *Herd: How to Change Mass Behavior by Harnessing Our True Nature* (New York: Wiley, 2007).
Freud, Sigmund. *Civilization and Its Discontents*, trans. James Strachey (London: Hogarth Press and Institute of Psychoanalysis, 1930; New York: W.W. Norton, 2010).
Hansen, Alvin. "Economic Progress and Declining Population Growth," *The American Economic Review*, 29(1) (March 1939): 1–15.
Kotklikoff, Laurence. *Jimmy Stewart is Dead: Ending the World's Ongoing Financial Plague with Limited Purpose Banking* (New York: John Wiley and Sons, 2010).

Marcuse, Herbert. *Soviet Marxism: A Critical Analysis* (New York: Columbia University Press, 1958).
Moszkowa, Natalia. *Zur Dynamik des Spätkapitalismus* (Zurich: Verlag der Aufbruch, 1943).
Riesman, David. *The Lonely Crowd: A Study in the Changing American Character* (New Haven, CT: Yale University Press, 1961).
Ross, Carne. *The Leaderless Revolution: How Ordinary People Will Take Power and Change Politics in the 21st Century* (New York: Blue Rider Press, 2012).
Slater, Philip. *The Pursuit of Loneliness: American Culture at the Breaking Point* (Boston, MA: Beacon Press, 1970).
Streeck, Wolfgang. *How Will Capitalism End? Essays on a Failing System* (London and New York: Verso, 2016).
Tufekci, Zeynep. "Does a Protest's Size Matter?" op-ed, *The New York Times*, January 27, 2017.
Tufekci, Zeynep. *Twitter and Tear Gas: The Power and Fragility of Networked Protest* (New Haven, CT: Yale University Press, 2017).
Turkle, Sherry. *Reclaiming Conversation: The Power of Talk in a Digital Age* (New York: Penguin, 2015).
Vujačić, Veljko. "Victor Zaslavsky's Contribution to the Study of Soviet-type Societies," *Ventunesimo Secolo*, 30 (February 2013): 193–204.
Wilkinson, Richard and Kate Pritchett. *The Spirit Level: Why More Equal Societies Almost Always Do Better* (London: Allen Lane, 2009).
Wikipedia, s.v. "Predistribution," last modified December 12, 2016, https://en.wikipedia.org/wiki/Predistribution.
Zaslavsky, Victor. *The Neo-Stalinist State* (Boston, MA: M.E. Sharpe, 1982).

4

The New Ancien Régime

According to the *Encyclopedia Britannica*, the term *Ancien Régime* ("old order") refers to the political and social system of France prior to the French Revolution. Its essence lies in the interweaving of the state's social, political, and economic forms; the term itself, though primarily a political concept, has also always had a clear social and economic resonance.

Privilege was at the very center of that society of orders known as Bourbon France. The privileges of the nobility, clergy, and king were only the apex of a structure of entitlements that reached into many provinces and affected nearly all cities and towns—in part, through the urban occupations organized into corporations. Toward the end of the Ancien Régime, criticisms of privilege as unfair, unjust, or unproductive were heard from all over the country. No one said it better or more effectively than the Abbé Sieyès whose polemic *Essai sur les privilèges* of 1788 helped to crystallize public sentiment on the eve of the convocation of the Estates General. He repeated the common assertion that privilege was "a dispensation or exemption in favor of him who possesses it and a discouragement to those who do not." Sieyès added "it is the essence, the characteristic, of privilege to place the possessor of it beyond the boundaries of common right."[1]

In his examination of the Ancien Régime, Alexis de Tocqueville made the important argument that the attempts at reforming the system only made matters worse: just as the municipal and judicial reforms of 1787–1788 removed the teeth of the Bourbon administration, leaving the intendants with few tools to combat growing instability, so too, expansions of the privilege of liberty in combination with limitations imposed by crushing debt meant that, in the short term, the French state could do little to ameliorate the economic crisis. In the end, it all crashed down in the upheaval of 1789.[2]

At first blush, nothing could be more distant and different from present-day globalization than eighteenth-century French society. The mode of production, the class structure, and the political regime are as far from today as a distant planet is from Earth. And yet, the Ancien Régime and twenty-first century globalization share an alarming similarity on a higher level of abstraction—that is, at the level of the structure and dynamics of systems. In both cases, the very functioning of the economy and society produced extreme inequality. In turn, such inequality—which could not be mitigated or reversed—became very visible and very difficult to justify. In short, in the eyes of vast swaths of the population, it became a regime of privileges with diminishing legitimacy.

As I have stated, in the case of France, critics launched a philosophically reasoned attack on the system that Abbé Sieyès had best exemplified in his *Essay on Privileges*. But in our more technical era of today, critics offer a reasoned economic argument against the regime, as discussed in Thomas Piketty's *Capital in the 21st Century* and Joseph Stiglitz's *The Price of Inequality*. In contemporary sociology, Charles Tilly possibly offered the best analysis in his book *Durable Inequality*. Tilly was also an expert on pre-revolutionary and revolutionary France, which provided an empirical jumping board for his theoretical disquisition. To the equation, *increased inequality=illegitimate privilege*, I would add another structural characteristic of Ancien Régimes. It is the inability of the elites to correct or steer the dysfunctions. Even worse, the very attempts to reform the system made its crisis more acute.

In the past few years, a spectrum haunts the snowy peaks of Switzerland: a growing social protest—still amorphous—is set against an increasingly dysfunctional and ill-formed globality. What are the signs of this protest? Who is scared by the primary mobilization of those moving up and the secondary mobilization of those moving down?

Every January in the Swiss Alpine village of Davos, the world elite gathers to discuss world affairs, and above all to see and to be seen.

The distinguished convocation consists of a hard core of those who manage big corporations and the financial system, and a few world leaders, surrounded by a chorus of sherpas, politicians, aspirants, publicists, scientists, accredited journalists, and some celebrities. In sum, it is an assembly of the powerful, the influential, and those aspiring to become so. As Hipólito Irigoyen—an Argentine president in the early part of the twentieth century—would say, it is the biggest *"cuspideo"* ("summitry") one can imagine. Besides discussing the latest novelties on communication and finance technology—as they have often done, the participants have become aware of a specter that runs through the corridors, causing concern and sometimes fear: the specter of people bemoaning the concentration of power and wealth, the lack of opportunities, and the precariousness of employment.[3] The rise of populism is associated with these structural shifts. In a recent paper, investor Ray Dalio developed a populism index with nine indicators and used it to produce this chart (Figure 4.1).[4]

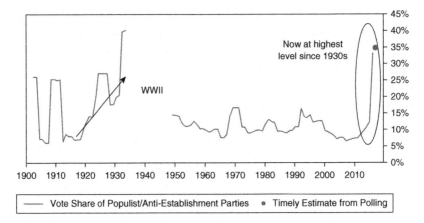

* The latest point includes cases like Trump, UKIP in the UK, AfD in Germany, National Front in France, Podemos in Spain, and Five Star Movement in Italy. It doesn't include major emerging country populists, like Erdogan in Turkey or Duterte in the Philippines. In the rest of the study, we look at populists of the past rather than those now in office in order to study the phenomenon because the stories of ones in power or possibly coming to power are still being written. For example, while we consider Donald Trump to be a populist, we have more questions than answers about him and are using these other cases to assess him against by seeing if he follows a more archetypical path or if he deviates from it significantly.

Figure 4.1   Developed World Populism Index*

© 2017 Bridgewater® Associates, LP.

Recent research on the rise of populism in the West indicates that cultural values are better predictors of voting for populist parties right and left than sheer economic deprivation, depending on the context. On the basis of cross-national survey data, political scientists Ronald Inglehart and Pippa Norris maintain that what is going on in the populist surge at the polls is a retro-reaction to progressive (liberal) value change.[5] In my own view, cultural variables are intervening rather than independent. Cultural attitudes are the product of life experiences, whereas long trends in economic insecurity are profoundly existential as they shake up confidence in progressive change when the system time and again fails to "deliver the goods," betraying promises of a better life for oneself and one's progeny.

As a seaman, I find the analogy with the study of weather systems apt to clarify my point. Just as a navigator needs to build a picture or comprehensive understanding of the weather, a sociologist needs to build a comprehensive picture of the large structural movements and shifts that drive culture and the experience of daily life. Just as the local weather conditions that we experience at the Earth's surface are related to air masses and fronts, the structural conditions far above us impact cultural movements. High in the atmosphere, bands of strong wind steer weather systems and transfer heat and moisture around the globe. Similarly, trends in the political economy drive perceptions and attitudes. The locations over which they form determine their characteristics. Robert K. Merton's classic study of the "American Dream" provides a comprehensive framework (strain theory[6]) to understand the range of adaptations in the cultural system to structural obstacles to social mobility—a fundamental component of which is what Max Weber called "market chances."

To well-groomed elites in complacent bubbles, the besieging crowds must look like zombies, like the walking dead from a bygone industrial era. Protests multiply; they are expressed in populism with right and left orientations, and in some countries, they threaten to take to office certain leaders who, for the established oligarchs, "are not people like us."

This chapter aims at characterizing some of these currents. In fact, the populace does not mind those elites who fulfill the proper terms of their position and display a degree of *noblesse oblige*—that is the active use of power for the betterment of the lives of everybody. During the

Great Depression, millions of impoverished Americans put their trust in Franklin Delano Roosevelt—the wealthy scion of an old patroon family of the Hudson Valley—for he spoke to their needs and acted in their behalf. Such politicians are not in evidence today. Ours is a period of aloof technocrats and brazen oligarchs. Populist adventurers understand this and wait in the wings. They are ready to replace the older liberal elites that have lost touch with Joe six-pack. In the 1940s, a paradigmatic national-populist, Juan Domingo Perón, put it succinctly, "Either we march at the head of the people or the people will march with our head on a pike."[7]

Today's great and increasing wealth inequality has multiple perverse effects, including those that affect the viability of the very system that produces such concentration. In the United States in 2007, on the verge of the financial crash and the ensuing Great Recession, 1 percent of the citizens had 34 percent of national wealth. The next 9 percent managed 38.5 percent, while 90 percent controlled the remaining 26.9 percent (as reported by the Federal Reserve). As of this writing, having meekly come out of the Big Recession, inequality is even worse.

In America, inequality has been accepted historically because it usually took place in a context of growth, with significant benefits accruing to the working class. That has changed, steadily and unpleasantly, throughout the preceding decades. After the last world war, the West enjoyed 30 years of growth and prosperity. The French refer to those years, from 1945 to 1975, as *"les trente glorieuses."* But they were followed by more than three inglorious and lackluster decades—*"les trente misérables."* In this century alone, per capita growth has been, on average, less than 1 percent a year. If the United States had been able to sustain the growth rates that it enjoyed after the Second World War into the twenty-first century, the per capita gross national product (GDP) would be more than 20 percent higher than it is today.

Based on various reliable sources, critical economist Joel Kotkin reports,

> By margins of more than two to one, more Americans believe that they enjoy fewer economic opportunities than their parents, and that they will have far less job security and disposable income. This pessimism is particularly intense among white working-class voters and large sections of the middle class.[8]

In other words, the proverbial rising tide continues to lift boats, but they are mostly mega yachts.[9]

The backsliding of both living standards and expectations is especially stark when we consider that capitalism has reached new heights in productivity and spews a superabundance of goods on the global market. From an economic point of view, this situation raises the challenge of an unmanageable surplus—unmanageable by the established system of social relations. Too much production on the one hand, weak demand on the other. Some economists like Larry Summers draw attention to the risk of a "secular stagnation." The system can only continue functioning by promoting irrational behaviors, such as producing stimuli with fiat money to counteract a floor of interest rates considered very low, null, or even negative; sumptuary investment bubbles, public and private indebtedness; corruption and money-laundering; and the tendency to "buy" not just political parties but entire political systems—democratic or not—in extremely expensive campaigns.

Last but not least, there is military expense—weapons and deterrence and destruction devices that are much more efficient in "burning surplus" than in dissuading subversive violence that spreads in a capillary and asymmetric way. Directly or indirectly, such investment generates employment and feeds an entire industry of death, vigilance, and persecution in an abstract and endless "war." Surveying the American military, although I observe the presence of learned and capable strategists in the higher ranks, the wars in which they must engage are absurd.[10] We are already living in a world of rigorous surveillance, albeit to little avail in terms of safety.

With the end of the Cold War and the closing of socialist systems—from the collapse of Soviet communism to China's conversion toward a state-steered capitalism—the globalized late capitalism, with all its contradictions, no longer has an external rival, an "Other" who confronts and threatens it; an opponent who could discipline it and force it to make concessions under penalty of losing points in the global geopolitical game. Today, this absolute power generates its own nemesis. It is a machine that works at full speed but without brakes. Without communists, militant unions, an old or a new left, or even the resistance of pre-capitalist cultures, late or "compleat" capitalism (meaning highly skilled and accomplished in all aspects; total)[11] has left only one enemy, an implacable and unbeatable enemy: itself. In this context, it seems apt to remember a premonitory statement from a radical critic in the days of the Weimar Republic:

> The notion of the class war can be misleading. It does not refer to a trial of strength to decide the question "Who shall win, who be defeated?" or to a struggle whose outcome is good for the victor and bad for the vanquished. To think in this way is to romanticize and obscure the facts. For whether the bourgeoisie wins or loses the fight, it remains doomed by the inner contradictions that in the course of development will become deadly.[12]

The main beneficiaries of globality—a miniscule group in demographic terms but trillion-rich in capital—care about the short term. With delaying tactics, they also care about some minor cosmetic reforms and, at the very best, about their most virtuous philanthropy. Socially, they are so isolated from common life that they turn a deaf ear to the growing outcry of those who, group after group, are left behind or left out. Their reaction to social protest reminds us of the words attributed to Marie Antoinette. "If they do not have bread, let them eat brioche." They prefer to note the progress in the living standard of huge Asian masses, mobilized during the last decades as an urban industrial proletariat with low incomes though higher than the miserable level they were accustomed to in rural areas. But what about the erstwhile home base of the system, what we can still call the rich West?

Of the two former communist giants, Russia has descended to the status of a large energy commodity exporter, with the deleterious social and political consequences that such export dependency entails.[13] The other giant, China, has taken a far more promising tack. China's process of primitive accumulation for the sake of a model of export-oriented industrialization represents an experiment in socio-productive integration without precedent in history. This growth model has produced deindustrialization at the center and industrialization at the periphery. However, the model—once called "Chimerica" during its splendor—has reached its limits. For example, China is currently focused on a new revolution: nothing less than a gigantic "export substitution" (to revert to Raul Prebisch's expression in reverse[14]) and a social adjustment in pursuit of both a service society and a better level of life. It seeks to forge a true and new middle class, with a large internal market for its production and an increase in the scale of value, added through a lower investment in hardware and a higher investment in knowledge, information, and communications. In summary, its strategy—still a long-term strategy—aims at transforming for good an ancient civilization into a vanguard nation.

It is possible that a future increase in Chinese demand will turn the country again into a growth locomotive for the world economy, but we would need to wait for China to first complete its projected internal social reconversion. By that time, Chinese resurgence will have caused geopolitical frictions with neighboring countries and with the declining but still huge power of the United States. Besides, before we heap premature praise on the achievements of China, we must note that capitalism in that country—"Adam Smith in Beijing"—while freeing hundreds of millions from poverty, has created the worst inequality in Asia (aside from Nepal). One percent of Chinese households are reported to enjoy 40 to 60 percent of total household wealth.[15]

In the meantime, the geopolitical competition continues, and the political turmoil in the United States may well hobble the nation in these sweepstakes. An old Chinese saying states, "People with petty shrewdness attend to trivial matters, while people with vision attend to governance of institutions." As the dysfunctionality of their political system distracts Americans, other powers advance. The commentator Thomas Friedman puts it in plain terms, "I wonder if the Chinese are spending their days this way. I suspect they've added another high-speed rail line just since Trump's election."[16] This merits a comparative reflection on the social origins of a capacity for long-term strategy.

In communist China, the bureaucratic system attained a kind of adaptability and capacity for experimentation that proved impossible in Soviet-type societies. Path dependency had a lot to do with it. Before coming to power, the Chinese communists controlled widely spread-out districts, leaving room for local initiatives. The Chinese Revolution was more dispersed and "bottom-up" than the Russian Revolution, which was *ab initio* centralized and top-down. In socialist societies, a fair degree of flexibility is a key to the longevity of regimes.

At least in the initial phases of development until the mid-2000s—the single party in power successfully set long-term strategies, both internally and externally, such as the modernization of industry, technology, and infrastructure planning on the domestic front, while it played, as Henry Kissinger has argued, a masterful game of go on the foreign front.

The twin perils for adaptive strategy are a brittle single party system that cannot allow for an alternation in power—hence the diffusion of blame in case of errors—and the natural tendency of the bureaucracy to become hidebound, thus a slow-down of experimentation. In Western democracies, the perils are almost symmetrical opposites of those in China, namely the incapacity for long-range strategy due to political polarization and gridlock, and the short-term nature of the electoral regime, reinforced by a narrow focus on shareholder profit in the private sector.

The problem the world is facing, the one that has already knocked on Davos's doors, is the following: if public policies in developed countries do not change from mere short-term monetary remedies to a medium- and long-term investment strategy in infrastructure and education, and a greater participation of the population in the new public and private sources of employment—or in their absence, a basic guaranteed income for all—the elites will have to address economic stagnation, distributive struggles, monetary wars and populist movements, and everything *in crescendo*. Imagine a world in which those at the top consume the surplus in luxury waste (like the conspicuous consumption of the Gilded Age) and those at the bottom, the "precariats," eke out a living, even though they are hooked on iPhones and androids. It would be a world in which social classes would have hardened into castes. That world could easily explode. Such is the real fear of the global elite in its snowy nest of January.

To understand the social dimension of the economic and geopolitical processes that I have just mentioned, I was able to count on Latin American sociological sources, whose intellectual father (at least in the Southern Cone) was Gino Germani.[17] In the 1960s, this astute

Italian-Argentinian sociologist presented a highly suggestive thesis of modernization. Faced with the problem of how to characterize Peronism in Argentina, Germani formulated a distinction between primary and secondary social mobilization. He was one of the first ones to argue that Peronism was a phenomenon different from European fascism. Germani's argument was that such political experience was a multi-class movement based on alliances between the new industrial bourgeoisie, an old and a new proletariat, and the military. The main accomplishment of that movement was to incorporate the lower classes into the productive system and sponsor their participation in the national political life. Thus, the composition and the goals of Peronism made it a phenomenon different from fascism.[18]

The social mobilization enters into play when old commitments as well as social, psychological, and political loyalties disintegrate, making different sectors of the population available to access new ways of behavior. However, it is important to stress the distinction that Germani held between primary and secondary mobilizations. Secondary mobilization frequently occurs as a reaction to the primary mobilization of sectors once excluded or marginalized. For example, when the old middle classes (already incorporated into the social and political system) feel threatened by the advancement of other groups (immigrants, minorities, and so on) or are affected by a prolonged economic crisis that carries the painful prospect of downward social mobility for them, they mobilize against the existing system and its new arrivers. In this case, their populism is, according to Germani, fascist in character. Fascism would be a reactionary movement that has turned popular. Today, new technologies of communication, which once were expected to provide more dialogue and enlightenment, have in fact produced the opposite. They can easily boost resentment and spur conflict. Social media may well be a misnomer. Some sociologists have gone as far as asserting that the new media are the medium of a "micro-fascism."[19]

During a crisis where ideological clarity is lost, social mobilization promotes odd pairings and strange bedfellows. From my perch, it is as comprehensible as it seems to be emotional and irrational. The underlying cause is the following. Late capitalism has reorganized the class structure in a globalized economy that is highly concentrated, with new and relatively small groups at the top, profiting from new technologies and from an "intangible" mode of production.[20] These new upper classes are progressive in social mores while benefitting from high incomes while easily tolerating the slow growth—the secular stagnation—of the system. In the United States, they are largely liberal and generally favor the Democratic Party. At the other end, the many blue- and white-collar workers that the older "tangible" industries (transportation, construction, energy, etc.) employ—once the bastion of the Democratic Party—are now the bulwark of Republican conservatives as well as the fertile ground for more extreme right-wing movements. What was going up is now coming down, and consequently, who was on the left is now on the right—and the reverse is true as well.

According to an analysis of the changing class structure in America and its political reflection, not only conservatism but liberalism, too, has made a U-turn.

> In the new formulation, the great *raison d'être* for left-wing politics—advocating for the middle and working classes—has been refocused to attend more closely to the policy imperatives and interests of small, highly affluent classes as well as the powerful public sector.[21]

The middle and working classes that are left behind are resentful and looking for alternatives, including the "alt-right." In short, the gentry on the left are elitist and globalist; the working class is populist and nationalist. The former has risen to unprecedented heights of wealth and privilege; the latter has declined in income and status and sees its dream of betterment betrayed.[22]

In the twentieth century, the 2008 financial collapse would have produced a massive street mobilization of left-wing parties, in particular the European Marxists. For these movements, revolution seemed to be within reach and their parties ready for power. But the twenty-first century, at least in its beginnings, seems to have lost the appetite for a radical and secular change. The failure of the Soviet system brought with it the international discredit of socialism, except for some so-called progressive Latin American bastions, riding a wave of good commodity prices for a while. In other latitudes, enthusiasm was succeeded by apathy; in others, protest, though violent, became retrograde, traditionalist, or religious. Almost a decade has passed since a crisis broke out that seemed terminal at one point, but from which the system "saved" itself with some emergency measures and, above all, from not having an organized opposition.

Today, these cosmetic solutions—the proverbial rabbits that the magician pulls out of his hat—seem exhausted. Elites do not ignore what could be done to save the system, but either they cannot or they do not dare to. For example, the European Union does not know how to carry a rational and consensual policy to regulate the refugee flow. In the United States, for many decades and for the sake of labor flexibility, the government and employers allowed a flow of undocumented immigrants—equivalent to today's entire Chilean population—into the country. President Obama's lukewarm attempts to regulate that mass of new arrivals and to rationalize the frontiers were systematically torpedoed by the right-wing opposition, and then given a *coup de grâce* by his successor, President Trump, the American *accabador*, with a bombastic promise to build a wall. Another example: it is clear that the European austerity policy was a complete failure. It is a pro-cyclical, and socially harmful, macro-economic policy. But the technocratic elite in Brussels stubbornly advocates that "in the long run" it will work, without remembering that famous quote by John M. Keynes, "in the long run we are all dead." A third evident example is the need to end the excessive financialization of the economy and control the financial and banking sectors. But who dares taunt this beast when it has managed to have so many politicians on its payroll? And the same can be said regarding the need to maintain competitive enterprises when the corruption of monopoly has spread everywhere, not to mention the need to establish a tax system that increases the contributions of the rich and powerful, who not only protect themselves through their "lobbies" but also have convinced the common taxpayer that rejecting any increase in taxes is a "patriotic act" as well. In summary: the reformist solution of the system is practically doable but politically impossible. It is like a steam boiler without an escape valve preparing for an explosion. In many ways it is the ultimate example of a strategic impasse.

In their inaction, the elites can contemplate a general yet varied protest, without rational organization and and mixing issues that previously separated the left from the right. This confusion feeds from the secondary mobilization of the unemployed youth as well as from the old declining middle class. In the twentieth century, a similar situation fed fascist movements in Europe. We can see how the same broth is brewed today and how protests spread throughout Europe.

Leftist political movements in Greece, Spain, and England—that is, such parties as *Syriza* in Greece, *Podemos* in Spain, and Corbyn's Labour party in the United Kingdom—propose the nationalization of industry and commerce control. But at the same time, the Brexit movement in Britain and the extreme right in France, gathered around Marine Le Pen's National Front (to mention just two of a growing number of right-wing movements), raise the same flags, adding a xenophobic and racist tenor to their demands. With political astuteness, the French National Front makes its annual festival on May 1st, traditionally a communist holiday in France. But today many old communists vote for the right. They are against globalization that has closed industries, and against immigration that brings "disloyal" labor competition. In Hungary, the right-wing government proposes to nationalize banks. The same thing is happening in Poland with its right-wing government that espouses a new economic nationalism. In England, the outspoken provocateur Nigel Farage, founder of the UKIP party, advocates increasing welfare expenditures while closing frontiers. In sum: issues from the old socialist left reemerge, but this time under a national flag. Is it patriotic neo-capitalism, neo-socialism, or old-fashioned National Socialism?

Faced with this specter, the global elite one day soon may long for the comfortable opposition of its old class enemies, now defunct. As capitalism reaches completion, it may begin to collapse from its own weight. In Timothy Garton Ash's words, "compleat" capitalism, or globality, is "not a new world order but a new world disorder. An unstable kaleidoscope world-fractured, overheated, germinating future conflicts."[23]

Liberal reformists, leftist protestors, and nationalist insurgents trade slogans and flags, and fight one another around a phenomenon that they do not fully understand but that continues apace and unabated. Techno-globalization will continue, and will accentuate the confusion.

The past is irretrievable, the present unsustainable, and the future, as the saying goes, is not what it used to be. To navigate these confused seas requires a clear head,[24] a strong stomach, and a lot of patience. All three are in short supply.[25] Compleat capitalism is experiencing the beginning of its end. What lies beyond? We are at "the end of the beginning" of new solutions, many tentative, some contradictory, and all cutting across old political and ideological divides.[26]

Today we would call Sieyès's Third Estate our civil society—in particular, productive workers and the productive middle class, threatened with downward mobility and marginalization. Inequality has increased so much in our own era that the Third Estate is the equivalent of what the protestors in "Occupy Wall Street" called "the 99 percent." Sieyès would be comfortable with their critique. His remarks of 1789 merit repetition in 2017:

> It suffices to have made the point that the so-called usefulness of a privileged order to the public service is a fallacy; that, without help from this order, all the arduous tasks in the service are performed by the Third Estate; that without this order the higher posts could be infinitely better filled; that they ought to be the natural prize and reward of recognized ability and service; and that if the privileged have succeeded in usurping all well-paid and honorific posts, this is both a hateful iniquity towards the generality of citizens and an act of treason to the commonwealth.
>
> Who is bold enough to maintain that the Third Estate does not contain within itself everything needful to constitute a complete nation? It is like a strong and robust man with one arm still in chains. If the privileged order were removed, the nation would not be something less but something more. What then is the Third Estate? All; but an "all" that is fettered and oppressed. What would it be without the privileged order? It would be all; but free and flourishing. Nothing will go well without the Third Estate; everything would go considerably better without the others.[27]

To repeat the point: at both the international and the national levels, elites seem unable to govern the commons. Even worse, the very attempts to reform the system often make its crises more pronounced. Under such strains, a serious disorganization, conflict, or loss of control at the top can open the sluice gates of a general insurrection, with different ideological tones, mixing futuristic utopias with reactionary attempts to return to the past. The present anti-global movements and the resurgence of national populisms are a case in point. They are components of a low-intensity general insurrection, still inchoate, and not necessarily rational. It could get worse. Welcome to the world in 2018.

Notes

1. Count Emmanuel Joseph Sieyès, *An Essay on Privileges, and Particularly on Hereditary Nobility*, trans. by a foreign nobleman (London: J. Ridgway, 1791), https://searchworks.stanford.edu/view/8088328.
2. Alexis de Tocqueville, *The Old Regime and the Revolution*, trans. John Bonner (New York: Harper & Brothers, 1856).
3. For a first take on the phenomenon, see Standing, *The Precariat*. Also see Eberstadt, *Men Without Work*.
4. Katia Porzenscanski, Bridgewater Associates and 2017 Report, www.bloomberg.com/news/articles/2017-03-22/dalio-says-populism-may-be-stronger-than-fiscal-monetary-policy. Since the dismal science has taken over macro-structural analysis from a distracted sociology, we must resort to research sponsored by enlightened businessmen to gauge some important trends.
5. Ronald F. Inglehart and Pippa Norris, "Trump, Brexit, and the Rise of Populism: Economic Have-nots and Cultural Backlash." Paper presented at the World Congress of the Political Science Association, Posnan, Poland, July 25, 2016.
6. Robert K. Merton, "Social Structure and Anomie," *American Sociological Review* 3(5) (October 1938): 672–682, and "Continuities in the Theory of Social Structure and Anomie," in *Social Theory and Social Structure* (New York: Free Press, 1968), 215–248.
7. The oft-quoted saying in Spanish was "*Con los dirigentes a la cabeza o con la cabeza de los dirigentes.*" Perón got his inspiration from Benito Mussolini, Huey Long, and Franklin Delano Roosevelt.
8. Kotkin, *The New Class Conflict*, 68.
9. It is not just a metaphor. I am a small sailboat owner living across from one of the largest shipyards for yachts in the United States, and can bear witness to the glamorous floating palaces docked across my front door. For an industry that caters to the new global oligarchs, see For latecomers to the

boating mega-rich, see Matthew DeBord, "The Largest Mega-yacht Ever Built in China Is Incredibly Luxurious," *Business Insider*, August 7, 2014, www.businessinsider.com/the-largest-mega-yacht-ever-built-in-china-is-incredibly-luxurious-2014-8. Also see Matt Spector, "World's Elite Make a Splash with Mega Yachts," ABC News, August 6, 2008.

10 The situation was anticipated in a radical reinterpretation of armed conflict by the Israeli military historian Martin Van Creveld, *The Transformation of War* (New York: Free Press, 1991). It is probably the most significant contribution to the field since Carl von Clausewitz.

11 An early and premonitory formulation of this stage appeared in Herbert Marcuse, *One Dimensional Man* (Boston, MA: Beacon Press, 1964). A more recent formulation, based on a survey of theories of capitalism, appears in Streeck, *How Will Capitalism End?* Another term for the completion of late capitalism is "globality," mentioned at the opening of this chapter. Wikipedia defines it as "the end-state of globalization—a hypothetical condition in which the process of globalization is complete or nearly so, barriers have fallen, and 'a new global reality' is emerging," https://en.wikipedia.org/wiki/Globality.

12 Walter Benjamin, *One-Way Street* (Cambridge and New York: Harvard University Press, 2016), 65.

13 See Michael Friedson, Leslie-Ann Bolden, and Juan E. Corradi, "Before the Natural Resource Boon: State-civil Society Relations and Democracy in Resource Rich Societies," *Journal of Third World Studies*, 2 (Fall 2013), www.researchgate.net/publication/286696579_Before_the_natural_resource_boon_State-civil_society_relations_and_democracy_in_resource_rich_societies.

14 On the concepts and economic contributions of Prebisch, see Edgar J. Dosman, *The Life and Times of Raul Prebisch 1901–1986* (Montreal: McGill-Queens University Press, 2008).

15 Reported by *Financial Times*, April 20, 2011.

16 Thomas L. Friedman, "Meet the 5 Trump Administrations," op-ed, *The New York Times*, February 22, 2017.

17 Gino Germani, *Estructura Social de la Argentina* (Buenos Aires: Raigal, 1955). Such studies are still sorely needed in the developed world.

18 Gino Germani, *Autoritarismo, Fascismo y Populismo Nacional* (Buenos Aires: Temas Grupo Editorial, 2003).

19 Richard Miskoici, "Notas Sobre o Microfascismo nas Redes Sociais," *Revista Cult-Uol*, March 3, 2017, http://revistacult.uol.com.br/home/redes-de-ressentimento-notas-sobre-o-microfascismo-nas-redes-sociais/.

20 The shift has long been announced by sociologists like Daniel Bell and Alain Touraine, and by cultural critics like Jean Baudrillard. See Alain Touraine, *The Post-Industrial Society. Tomorrow's Social History: Classes, Conflicts and Culture in the Programmed Society* (New York: Random House, 1971); Daniel Bell, *The Coming of Post-Industrial Society. A Venture in Social Forecasting* (New York: Basic Books, 1973); Jean Baudrillard, *Modernes et Après. Les Immateriaux* (Paris: Editions Autrement, 1985).
21 Kotkin, *The New Class Conflict*, 9.
22 For a rather moving personal account of a forgotten corner of the United States where white Americans feel powerless, as their way of life is devastated, see J.D. Vance, *Hillbilly Elegy: A Memoir of a Family and Culture in Crisis* (New York: Harper Collins, 2016). It is the closest equivalent for our times to the 1930s classic *Let Us Now Praise Famous Men* by James Agee and Walker Evans.
23 Carne Ross, "Timothy Garton Ash in Davos: Illiberal Capitalism and New World Disorder," in *The Leaderless Revolution*, 7. For an earlier diagnosis see Juan E. Corradi, *Los Hilos del Desorden* (Buenos Aires: Ediciones Del Umbral, 2006).
24 An interesting take on past and present trends in the forces that drive globalization is by Richard Baldwin, *The Great Convergence. Information Technology and the New Globalization* (Cambridge, MA: Harvard University Press, 2016).
25 Perhaps the one positive result of the electoral "surprise" in the United States is a wake-up call to focus attention on the large problem of surplus populations—not just an aging and retired labor force but a vast army of the able-bodied who cannot find proper jobs.
26 For a small sample of proposals, consider Eberstadt, *Men Without Work*, Chapters 10–13; Standing, *The Precariat*, Chapters 6 and 7; Kotkin, *The New Class Conflict*, Chapter 7; Ross, *The Leaderless Revolution*, Chapters 7–9; and Thomas Piketty *et al.*, "For a Credible and Bold Basic Income," *Le Monde*, January 2017, http://piketty.blog.lemonde.fr/2017/01/25/pour-un-revenu-universel-credible-et-ambitieux/. For more information on basic income proposals, see Basic Income Earth Network, http://basicincome.org/; for Spanish speakers, the following cartoon: "¿Qué es la renta básica?," YouTube video, 5:11, posted by RedRentaBasica on February 10, 2017, www.youtube.com/watch?v=0WeB9ppG8kM; and for those who like TED Talks, see Sebastian Johnson, "The Case for Basic Income," YouTube video, 10:00, posted by TED Talks on January 13, 2017,

www.youtube.com/watch?v=H3YbZs-tu-I. For a more provocative proposal, see Roberto Sansón Mizrahi's "Dignity Trust: Open Letter to Eight People Whose Wealth is Equivalent to the Assets Held by 3.6 Billion People in Our Planet," *Opinion Sur*, March 23, 2017, http://opinionsur.org.ar/wp/dignity-trust/?lang=en.
27 Sieyès, *An Essay on Privileges*.

References

Agee, James and Walker Evans. *Let Us Now Praise Famous Men: Three Tenant Families* (1936, repr., New York: Houghton Mifflin Harcourt, 2001).

Baldwin, Richard. *The Great Convergence. Information Technology and the New Globalization* (Cambridge, MA: Harvard University Press, 2016).

Basic Income Earth Network, http://basicincome.org/; for Spanish speakers, the following cartoon: "*¿Qué es la renta básica?*," YouTube video, 5:11, posted by RedRentaBasica on February 10, 2017, www.youtube.com/watch?v=0WeB9ppG8kM.

Baudrillard, Jean. *Modernes et Après. Les Immateriaux* (Paris: Editions Autrement, 1985).

Bell, Daniel. *The Coming of Post-Industrial Society. A Venture in Social Forecasting* (New York: Basic Books, 1973).

Benjamin, Walter. *One-Way Street* (Cambridge and New York: Harvard University Press, 2016).

Corradi, Juan E. *Los Hilos del Desorden* (Buenos Aires: Ediciones Del Umbral, 2006).

DeBord, Matthew. "The Largest Mega-yacht Ever Built in China Is Incredibly Luxurious," *Business Insider*, August 7, 2014, www.businessinsider.com/the-largest-mega-yacht-ever-built-in-china-is-incredibly-luxurious-2014-8.

Dosman, Edgar J. *The Life and Times of Raul Prebisch 1901–1986* (Montreal: McGill-Queens University Press, 2008).

Eberstadt, Nicholas. *Men Without Work: America's Invisible Crisis* (West Conshohocken, PA: Templeton Press, 2016).

Financial Times, April 20, 2011.

Friedman, Thomas L. "Meet the 5 Trump Administrations," op-ed, *The New York Times*, February 22, 2017.

Friedson, Michael, Leslie-Ann Bolden and Juan E. Corradi. "Before the Natural Resource Boon: State-civil Society Relations and Democracy in Resource Rich Societies," *Journal of Third World Studies*, no. 2 (Fall 2013).

Germani, Gino. *Autoritarismo, Fascismo y Populismo Nacional* (Buenos Aires: Temas Grupo Editorial, 2003).

Germani, Gino. *Estructura Social de la Argentina* (Buenos Aires: Raigal, 1955).

Inglehart, Ronald F. and Pippa Norris. "Trump, Brexit, and the Rise of Populism: Economic Have-nots and Cultural Backlash." Paper presented at the World Congress of the Political Science Association, Posnan, Poland, July 25, 2016.

Johnson, Sebastian. "The Case for Basic Income," YouTube video, 10:00, posted by TED Talks on January 13, 2017, www.youtube.com/watch?v=H3Yb Zs-tu-I.

Kotkin, Joel. *The New Class Conflict* (New York: Telos Press, 2014).

Marcuse, Herbert. *One Dimensional Man* (Boston, MA: Beacon Press, 1964).

Merton, Robert K. "Social Structure and Anomie," *American Sociological Review* 3(5) (October 1938): 672–682.

Merton, Robert K. "Continuities in the Theory of Social Structure and Anomie," in *Social Theory and Social Structure* (New York: Free Press, 1968).

Miskoici, Richard. "Notas Sobre o Microfascismo nas Redes Sociais," *Revista Cult-Uol*, March 3, 2017, http://revistacult.uol.com.br/home/redes-de-ressentimento-notas-sobre-o-microfascismo-nas-redes-sociais/.

Mizrahi, Roberto Sanson. "Dignity Trust: Open Letter to Eight People Whose Wealth is Equivalent to the Assets Held by 3.6 Billion People in Our Planet," *Opinion Sur*, March 23, 2017, JEC1-04_Chapter 4.docx, http://opinionsur.org.ar/wp/dignity-trust/?lang=en.

Piketty, Thomas. *Capital in the 21st Century* (Cambridge, MA: Harvard University Press, 2014).

Piketty, Thomas *et al.* "For a Credible and Bold Basic Income," *Le Monde*, January 2017, http://piketty.blog.lemonde.fr/2017/01/25/pour-un-revenu-universel-credible-et-ambitieux/.

Porzenscanski, Katia, Bridgewater Associates and 2017 Report. "Ray Dalio Says Populism May Be a Bigger Deal Than Monetary and Fiscal Policy," www.bloomberg.com/news/articles/2017-03-22/dalio-says-populism-may-be-stronger-than-fiscal-monetary-policy.

Ross, Carne. *The Leaderless Revolution: How Ordinary People Will Take Power and Change Politics in the 21st Century* (New York: Blue Rider Press, 2011).

Sieyès, Count Emmanuel Joseph. *An Essay on Privileges, and Particularly on Hereditary Nobility*, trans. by a foreign nobleman (London: J. Ridgway, 1791), https://searchworks.stanford.edu/view/8088328.

Spector, Matt. "World's Elite Make a Splash with Mega Yachts," *ABC News*, August 6, 2008, http://abcnews.go.com/Travel/Weather/story?id=5518446&page=1.

Standing, Guy. *The Precariat: The New Dangerous Class* (London: Bloomsbury Group, 2016).

Stiglitz, Joseph. *The Price of Inequality* (New York: W.W. Norton, 2012).

Streeck, Wolfgang. *How Will Capitalism End? Essays on a Failing System* (London and New York: Verso, 2016).

Tilly, Charles. *Durable Inequality* (Berkeley, CA: University of California Press. 1999).

de Tocqueville, Alexis. *The Old Regime and the Revolution*, trans. John Bonner (New York: Harper & Brothers, 1856).

Touraine, Alain. *The Post-Industrial Society. Tomorrow's Social History: Classes, Conflicts and Culture in the Programmed Society* (New York: Random House, 1971).

Van Creveld, Martin. *The Transformation of War* (New York: Free Press, 1991).

Vance, J.D. *Hillbilly Elegy: A Memoir of a Family and Culture in Crisis* (New York: Harper Collins, 2016).

5
THE MINDLESS MIND, OR THE NEW WILES OF PROPAGANDA

Until the advent of social media and the new technologies of communication, propaganda was a tool used by states since the days in which the state system was established after the peace of Westphalia in 1648. To rally support among the underlying population and to broadcast their views abroad to other rival states, governments used biased information and disinformation.

As modern systems of control evolved and technology advanced to the era of mass media, propaganda expanded its scope and deepened its penetration of the public sphere.[1] Among other things, this process went hand in hand with the concentration of communication posts in a few large media organizations and reached its zenith with the emergence of total state control over information and ideology. New totalitarian systems, right and left, perfected these controls. With the near total elimination of alternative and dissenting positions, these totalitarian systems could affect, unchallenged, the ears, eyes, and minds of captive populations. Freedom of expression survived only in liberal democracies where there remained a fairly lively competition among differing views on policy, values, and rights. Except between liberal democracies, news and opinions had a hard time crossing borders. Totalitarian states sealed information in a lock box and kept their populations from entertaining positions contrary to the interests and objectives of the regimes in power.

Today, we live in a different world; a world that transcends borders and that promotes the free exchange of people, information, and products in a dense web of global networks of communication, production and distribution chains—and ideas as well. Very few states, like North Korea, are completely sealed off, and all states have a hard time monopolizing ideologies and facts.

But here is the rub: we no longer have to live in a dictatorship or closed society to be the victim of misinformation and propaganda. They can intrude on our homes, places of work, classrooms, and on the streets, as most of us are "glued" to the little screens of our smartphones. They can play with our minds and saturate our thoughts in ways that even the Reich Minister of Propaganda (1933–1945), Dr. Joseph Goebbels, could not have dreamed of.[2] Such devices were not imagined by the great dystopians of the twentieth century: Yevgeny Zamyatin, George Orwell, and Aldous Huxley. Theirs was the world of Big Brother and other fictional monsters of state. The publishing and movie industries produced thrillers and semi-documentaries featuring devilish schemes, spies and agents; from the long popular series of James Bond to critical films like *The Lives of Others*[3] and *Goodbye Lenin!*[4]

Nowadays, minds can be muddled, and often are, in the "private" world of a teenager's room. Silly news, false alarms, and factoids are beamed to a bored child in a classroom, or to a distracted passenger on a subway seat. The dystopia of our days could be labeled "tweets for twits." Thus, in a gentle and liquid way,[5] we are misled by new modes of propaganda.[6]

In my view, the oft-mentioned phenomenon of "fake news" is a communication strategy that operates on two levels. The first is the news itself, which seeks to dupe the receiver into believing something that is demonstrably false. The second level is more insidious. Even if the first level is debunked by fact checking as fake news, the second level operates as a meta-message *to distrust all news.*[7] The aim of propaganda at this level is to sow cynicism and produce a spurious equivalence between the true and the false. It is an instance of what Barrington Moore Jr. called "a vested interest in confusion."[8] As Goebbels knew well, the aim of propaganda is not to generate belief but to produce dis-orientation.[9] Social media is an ideal medium to practice such tactics. The strategy behind the tactics is to instill in crowds (physical or virtual) a readiness to jump in a leap of faith, and eventually to follow a strong leader. It is the secular version of an old dictum in Tertullian's work *De Carne Christi* (203–206 CE), "*prorsus credibile est, quia ineptum est,*" which can be translated as "it is by all means to be believed because it is absurd."

Social media can lead subjects into a realm of political hallucination. When liquid contact substitutes genuine conversation, political discourse develops an elective affinity for what, in the early years of mass culture, Walter Benjamin called the "phantasmagoria of commodities."[10] Already in the nineteenth century in London and Paris, "phantasmagoria" was a form of horror theater that used one or more magic lanterns to project frightening images—such as ghosts, skeletons, and demons—onto walls or screens, using rear projection to keep the lantern out of sight. This is no longer a quaint curiosity in our age of television, computers, and social media: a press conference in the Trump White House is often a re-edition of the old horror theater—with social media having replaced magic lanterns.

Most recent analyses on the current wiles of propaganda in an era of social media are good at diagnosing and illustrating the issues at stake but somewhat vague in the solutions proposed. Many of the proposed remedies focus quite appropriately on education. It is appalling that civics has been dropped from most curricula in primary and secondary education in the United States. At the college level, the need to cram courses that promise to hone practical abilities and prepare the student for an uncertain job market tend to displace the traditional liberal arts, focusing on a general awareness of the legacy of Western and non-Western civilizations. What these and other courses in the older liberal arts curriculum offer is the opportunity to exercise critical analysis and, above all, discernment in front of complex social and philosophical issues as well as the basics of a scientific ethos of critical inquiry and evaluation of facts. The protest against this lamentable state of affairs generally comes from conservative quarters, while more liberal minds tend to view the curriculum as being old fashioned and dismiss it in favor of often frivolous discourses on post-modernity, relativism, and sexual variations. Yet, it is precisely the traditions of modern inquiry and classic formulations that need to be preserved—not as museum artifacts but as living documents to help us navigate our own confused cultural waters.

Alarmed at the inability to judge the quality of news and the veracity of facts, many US schools are beginning to teach students about credible sourcing on social media. So far it consists of nothing more than informing consumers of food about ingredients—a latter-day version of *caveat emptor*. Some pedagogues propose adding fact-checking tools to the armamentarium of revamped civics courses.[11] It is a start but a weak one. Perhaps a better way would be to dissect (yes, even to deconstruct) the dialogues Socrates had with the sophists on the dusty road from Athens to the port of Piraeus that Plato reported on some time ago. These dialogues are a true workout for the mind in the gymnasium of reason. Do this early and often, and start at a very young age, as Sherry Turkle suggests in her book on reclaiming conversation in a digital age. But the issue is larger and wider than conversations in and out of school.

Under late capitalism, consumption (of objects, services, and ideas) and production (of objects, services, and ideas) blend together into an amalgam of spurious freedom—the freedom of *homo oeconomicus* to choose. Freedom and necessity are one, leisure and work are hard to distinguish from each other, rationality and irrationality are interchangeable, and alternatives coexist on the same plane.

In its late phase, the system has colonized the surrounding world on a one-sided non-orientable surface—as with a Möbius strip. I will mention only one segment of the strip, for it goes to the heart of the present political economy. When the system is its own ideology,[12] there is no need for propaganda to lead people in a certain direction. It suffices that they follow the rules of the game, and keep on playing it, time and again.

In another chapter, I mention inequality and insecurity as features of our age. Capital and labor are engaged in a new relationship. In the present context, it is worth noticing that not all members of the precariat are low-income earners. Some make an adequate living as part of the new workforce. What has changed—and it is sociologically significant—is the kind of management and control of the workforce. New "gig economic platforms," service companies like Uber, Lyft, and popular delivery services like Postmates, use novel approaches to induce workers to produce more. They rely on platform-mediated work to accomplish their corporate goals. So do companies and individuals posting assignments on crowdsourcing sites like Amazon Mechanical Turk, where a legion of workers earn piece-rate wages by completing discrete tasks.[13]

In the old days of industrialism, many companies used insights from social science to get more out of their workers. But those workers were located at the point of production. Industrial speed-up, immortalized by Charlie Chaplin in the film *Modern Times* and well known to sociologists of that era from the Hawthorne experiments, were industrial speed-up techniques aimed at extracting more surplus value from direct producers.[14] As the labor movement developed, unions forced capitalists to provide greater worker protection, and together with governments imposed minimum wages and overtime pay. Today, such tug-of-war between labor and capital is being replaced by a different mode of control of a nominally freer labor force, composed of independent agents who work part time or with variable rates of involvement and speed.

To achieve corporate profit goals, companies then resort to techniques that hitherto were applied only to consumers. In the past, from the days of *The Hidden Persuaders* onward,[15] companies nudged consumers into buying their products and services through advertisement and psychological tricks. The novelty today is that similar techniques are applied to producers. Companies use data and algorithms to exploit psychological tendencies and channel workers' behavior in the direction they want them to go. Freedom has become a form of social control, without a whiff of coercion. The objective is to get workers to internalize the company's goals. As videogame designers know well, internalized motivation is a powerful tool.

Capitalism has finally managed to colonize the mind at the very point of production. Manipulation of consumption and manipulation of production form a seamless web, a twenty-first century version of David Riesman's "other directed" and Herbert Marcuse's "one dimensional" individuals.

Power Redefined

In the networked world, the bases of power are shifting, and this shift demands new concepts. In other sections of this book, I argue that the so-called liberal world order (or architecture), designed (largely by the enlightened self-interest of the United States) after the Second World

War, is rapidly eroding before our eyes, and that "soft power"—that is the persuasion of ideology—is obsolete as initially defined. The reasons are several, some of them compelling.

Globalization has paradoxical effects. On the one hand it connects everybody and everything in a web of affiliations and supply chains. On the other hand, far from unifying humanity around a set of shared values and practices, and consolidating a rational and reasonable universe of discourse, it promotes division and fragmentation. As self-referential virtual "tribes" proliferate, so does conflict, which does not encounter mediating mechanisms in the very medium that connects so many users. Globalization also means that big tech companies can easily outmatch the agencies of state—elected or appointed officials, democratic or not—and therefore bypass the borders of countries hitherto organized into sovereign states.

Nation-states are Leviathans—big and small—that have been around since the seventeenth century. For the last three decades, they seemed capable of keeping up with the globalizing trend—mostly propelled by technology—by creating blocs and unions and by surrendering some sovereignty to supranational entities. But these larger units have proven dysfunctional on several levels, such as, the democratic accountability and proximity to constituents; the mitigation of social and regional inequalities; fiscal consolidation; and the management of economic crises. As a result, a resistance to and, in many cases, an outright rejection of globalization by swaths of the population is now widespread. Its first—and I believe temporary—manifestation is a return to nationalism, this time with a populist and anti-elite flavor.

At first blush, authoritarian leaders seem to proliferate like maggots on the corpses of the liberal world order and its ideological successor, neo-liberalism. "Illiberal democracy" and more conventional dictatorships are sprouting up everywhere. Hungary, Poland, Egypt, Turkey, Russia, China, the Philippines, Venezuela are just a motley sample of lands where the authoritarian trend is loud and clear. In the future, they may be joined, alas, by the homelands of the Enlightenment: France and the United States. Yet the reaction is unviable for a number of reasons.

The nationalist revival plants in the heads of its followers a dream of the renaissance of hard power. In China and Russia, the nationalist sentiment is strong. It is paramount in America. The mighty US military remains unmatched by all rivals combined and will be preeminent in the foreseeable future. But how many wars has America "won" since the Second World War? Its campaigns have been inconclusive at best and disastrous at worst.[16]

Nationalism may temporarily disrupt but cannot stop the advance of interconnection; it may hark back to, and perhaps provoke, interstate rivalries and conflicts, but interstate solidarities and intrastate divisions will hobble it. Finally, it may dethrone some elites but will replace them with other elites—who are initially more authoritarian. Eventually, "kinder, gentler" ones will take over. They are much more influential than conventional "strong leaders." For example, the founder of Facebook, Mark Zuckerberg, recently embarked on a multistate tour and launched a "conversation" with the American people; and in an open letter to the 1.8 billion Facebook users worldwide, Mr. Zuckerberg announced that he wishes to found a "global community." His ambitions go well beyond making sidereal sums of money. He invites the entire planet to jump into his playpen.

In short, the old Leviathan is faltering, and a new Behemoth is replacing it—a Behemoth "lite," a philanthropic ogre that acts like the puppeteer of disorder.[17] In all revolutions—abrupt or prolonged, violent or peaceful, left or right—those who surge, those who lead, and those who benefit are different sets.[18] The same will happen with the antiglobalization movements.

What is at play is a new technology of control that is neither coercive nor persuasive, but smoothly manipulative. It is the capacity to gather, analyze, and use information about people (something states have always done, but now is done by private organizations and at lightning speed) to move them in certain directions, or to nudge them toward some predetermined action. No politician or administrative spook can look into consumers' or voters' heads (that distinction is also being erased) like Amazon, Google, or Facebook can. The big tech companies have been tracking the wants, desires, dreams, and apprehensions of millions as they happen in real time, and they can—if they wish—shape them. Non-democratic governments have adopted some of these techniques as they monitor their societies in order to detect signs of unrest. But the monitoring devices are not supple enough and can be circumvented. No steel or railway tycoon of the bygone era of robber barons had as much power—outside of influencing or buying political outcomes—as the new tech giants have in reorienting behavior. The technology penetrates every aspect of business and production: from goods to services, from health management to education. Its power is neither traditionally hard nor traditionally soft, although it comes closer to the latter. It penetrates the sphere of work, without infringing on freedom of action. The new tech platforms put truth and fiction, genuine and false news, information and entertainment on the same Möbius plane. While using science, they can manipulate science in ways no "Aryan physics" or "Lysenko genetics" ever did. Old truths are rediscovered and uncomfortable truths rapidly forgotten.

"Give me a place to stand and with a lever I will move the whole world" was not only Archimedes's application of mechanics, but it was also the stance of independent thinkers like John Stuart Mill. Today, places to stand and levers to move are hard to find—except perhaps in corporate headquarters. Propaganda has developed subtle wiles. Neither enforced silence (as in authoritarian regimes) nor command performance (as in fascist ones) will work in the networked world. Texting, Tweeting, Instagraming, and the mass forwarding of messages will.

The purport of this chapter has been to show that in the twenty-first, as opposed to the twentieth century, totalitarian tendencies are not necessarily limited to political centralization. Because of the new forms of propaganda, contemporary totalitarianism, which I believe is on the rise, is marked by what Barrington Moore Jr. foresaw many years ago—namely "a more diffuse conformity to repressive and irrational standards of behavior. Through an atmosphere of fear and suspicion, one sector of society is able to manipulate individual fears and aggressions to its own advantage."[19]

Notes

1 For a comprehensive study, see Jason Stanley, *How Propaganda Works* (Princeton, NJ: Princeton University Press, 2015).
2 For the technological opportunities and limitations in Goebbels's time, see his speech on propaganda, delivered in 1934, in which he anticipates the arrival of television (but of course not the Internet): "Joseph Goebbels on Propaganda 1934," History Wiz, www.historywiz.com/primarysources/goebbels.htm.

3. Florian Henckel von Donnersmarck. *The Lives of Others*. Directed by Florian Henckel von Donnersmarck (Munich, Germany: Wiedemann & Berg Film, 2006). A film about the monitoring of East Berlin residents by agents of the Stasi, the GDR's secret police.
4. Wolfgang Becker and Bernd Lichtenberg *et al*. Directed by Wolfgang Becker (Berlin, Germany, 2003). In 1990, to protect his fragile mother from a fatal shock after a long coma, a young man must keep her from learning that her beloved nation of East Germany, as she knew it, has disappeared.
5. Zygmunt Baumann used the term "liquid" in a series of papers and books like *Liquid Modernity* to describe a post-postmodern condition in which permanence gives way to transience, need to desire, and necessity to utility.
6. General Stanley McChrystal, "Save PBS: It Makes Us Safer," op-ed, *The New York Times*, April 5, 2017. Even an advocate of swift "hard power" urges the United States to maintain and expand the public broadcasting system as an antidote to commercially-driven media.
7. In a recent study on fake news and the 2016 US presidential election, academics Hunt Allcott and Matthew Gentzkow come to the conclusion that fake news was not directly game-changing: "for fake news to have changed the outcome of the election, a single fake article would need to have had the same persuasive effect as 36 television campaign ads." Hunt Allcott and Matthew Gentzkow, "Social Media and Fake News in the 2016 Election," *Journal of Economic Perspectives* 31(2) (Spring 2017): 211–236. My point is that the real effect of fake news is *to discredit news in general*—a sort of Gresham's law of information.
8. Barrington Moore Jr., *Political Power and Social Theory*, revised ed. (New York: Harper Torchbooks, 1965), 20.
9. Principle No. 16 of Goebbels's Manual of Propaganda states: "Propaganda to the home front must create an optimum anxiety level." See Leonard W. Doob, "Goebbels' Principles of Propaganda," in Daniel Katz *et al*. eds., *Public Opinion and Propaganda: A Book of Readings Edited for The Society for the Psychological Study of Social Issues* (1954, repr., New York: Holt, Rinehart and Winston, 1965).
10. Walter Benjamin, *Passagenwerk* (1927–1940), translated as *The Arcades Project*, trans. Howard Eiland and Kevin McLaughlin (Cambridge, MA: Harvard University/Belknap Press, 2002).
11. See the proposals by Tom Boll of Syracuse University's Newhouse School of Journalism. Cyndi Moritz, "Newhouse Professor Explains Fake News," Syracuse University News, January 24, 2017, https://news.syr.edu/2017/01/newhouse-professor-explains-fake-news/.

12 Max Horkheimer and Theodor W. Adorno, *Dialectics of Enlightenment* (1944, repr., Palo Alto/Redwood City, CA: Stanford University Press, 2002 and 2007). Horkheimer and Adorno anticipated this when they wrote that in advanced industrial society the noise of the machine had replaced the voices of ideology. Today, that noise has been replaced by the silent fingering of a little screen.
13 See Noam Scheiber, "How Uber Pushes Drivers' Buttons: Borrowing Video Game Tactics to Urge More Time on the Road," *The New York Times*, April 3, 2017.
14 See the classic report by Elton Mayo, "Hawthorne and the Western Electric Company," in *The Social Problems of an Industrial Civilization* (1945, repr., London: Routledge and Kegan Paul, 1949).
15 Vance O. Packard, *The Hidden Persuaders* (New York: Van Rees Press, 1957).
16 Vietnam and Iraq were appalling humiliations of American hard power. In 2005, the celebrated Israeli military historian Martin van Creveld wrote that the 2003 American invasion of Iraq was "the most foolish war since Emperor Augustus in 9 CE sent his legions into Germany and lost them" (Martin van Creveld, in a reference to the "Varian Disaster" that took place in the Forest of Teutoburg, when an alliance of Germanic tribes ambushed and decisively destroyed three Roman legions and their auxiliaries. I prefer to use a comparison with the Napoleonic disaster in Russia in 1812. Iran was the real victor in Iraq.
17 See Corradi, *Los Hilos del Desorden*.
18 I first came to this realization many years ago, on the occasion of a detailed study of the French Revolution that I carried out for a seminar on class and politics, conducted at Harvard University by Barrington Moore Jr. Since then, further studies of more cases have supported the initial hypothesis.
19 Barrington Moore Jr., "Totalitarian Elements in Pre-industrial Societies," in *Political Power and Social Theory*, 36.

References

Allcott, Hunt and Matthew Gentzkow. "Social Media and Fake News in the 2016 Election," *Journal of Economic Perspectives* 31(2) (Spring 2017): 211–236.

Bauman, Zygment. *Liquid Modernity* (Cambridge: Polity, 2000).

Benjamin, Walter. *Passagenwerk* (1927–1940), translated as *The Arcades Project*, trans. Howard Eiland and Kevin McLaughlin (Cambridge, MA: Harvard University/Belknap Press, 2002).

Corradi, Juan E. *Los Hilos del Desorden* (Buenos Aires: Ediciones Del Umbral, 2006).

Horkheimer, Max and Theodor W. Adorno. *Dialectics of Enlightenment* (1944, repr., Palo Alto/Redwood City, CA: Stanford University Press, 2002 and 2007).

Katz, Daniel *et al.* eds. *Public Opinion and Propaganda: A Book of Readings Edited for The Society for the Psychological Study of Social Issues* (1954, repr., New York: Holt, Rinehart and Winston, 1965).

Mayo, Elton. "Hawthorne and the Western Electric Company," in *The Social Problems of an Industrial Civilization* (1945, repr., London: Routledge and Kegan Paul, 1949).

McChrystal, General Stanley. "Save PBS: It Makes Us Safer," op-ed, *The New York Times*, April 5, 2017.

Moore, Barrington Jr. *Political Power and Social Theory*, revised ed. (New York: Harper Torchbooks, 1965).

Moritz, Cynid. "Newhouse Professor Explains Fake News," Syracuse University News, January 24, 2017, https://news.syr.edu/2017/01/newhouse-professor-explains-fake-news/.

Packard, Vance O. *The Hidden Persuaders* (New York: Van Rees Press, 1957).

Scheiber, Noam. "How Uber Pushes Drivers' Buttons: Borrowing Video Game Tactics to Urge More Time on the Road," *The New York Times*, April 3, 2017.

Turkle, Sherry. *Reclaiming Conversation* (New York: Penguin Press, 2015).

Van Creveld, Martin. *The Transformation of War* (New York: The Free Press, 1991).

6

ANOTHER RUBICON?

Reflections on Defeasance in the West

In the second decade of the twenty-first century, the United States faces the most significant shift in great-power relations since the collapse of the Soviet Union. As the current administration in Washington represents a change in regime in the United States, the geopolitical consequences will be epochal as well. What passes for a new set of policies is being sold as an American revival, but amounts in fact to a belligerent and fitful decadence. There are deep economic, social, and political forces propelling the decline. Some of the details are the subject of other chapters in this book. Here, I wish to share some comparative hypotheses that were prompted by a visit to the ruins of ancient Western splendor.

In January 2017, I took a vacation from American reality—or unreality—in Italy; among the Greco-Roman ruins of Paestum, I reflected on the present geopolitical predicament. Paestum was a city founded by Greek (Achaean) colonists. Its striking temples are still intact after more than 2,500 years of natural disasters and social upheavals. When the Romans took over, they dedicated one of these temples to *Mens Bona*—the Roman deity of reason, called upon to supervise the capacity for discernment of the political class. This was between the second and first centuries BCE, when Rome was a republic run by an oligarchy that sought to be wise. But things changed significantly—and ominously—after the "Roman Revolution,"[1] and the establishment of the empire. Historians are in general agreement that the pivotal moment was the *coup d'état* staged by Julius Caesar in 49 BCE when he marched on Rome at the head of his army.

Unwittingly perhaps, in the presidential election of 2016, American voters triggered their own sort of *coup d'état*. A democratic *coup d'état*? The expression sounds absurd, and yet, I shall explain how on some level it makes sense. It is, of course, not a classic *coup* of the abrupt military sort that we read about in the practical manuals of Curzio Malaparte and Edward Luttwak,[2] and which I witnessed in Argentina much too often.[3] It is rather a process in slower motion and in several stages, following a logic that operates behind the backs of the actors—the cunning of perverse reason, as in a Shakespearean tragedy or in a heavier Hegelian disquisition.

Faced with a choice of two controversial candidates, and through the convoluted process of indirect election, Americans produced a strange result that left millions perplexed. Now they have to live with an unpredictable outsider who has challenged the establishments of both major parties and who may succeed in demolishing the institutional fabric of the Republic as it was established in the late eighteenth century—a true *accabador*, as I explain in what follows.

The Hour of the *Accabadors*. Nationalism, Fragmentation, and Strategic Distraction in Europe

In the month of May, I sailed on a small sailboat along the coasts of Italy, from the Gulf of Venice to the Bay of Naples—that is, from the Adriatic to the Ionian to the Tyrrhenian seas. I visited numerous small ports, most of them charming, with echoes of a life without stress and with simpler values that are quickly fading from the world. These are the still traditional ways of life that for centuries were the backdrop—but also the sustaining soil—of a more dynamic modernizing capitalism in the urban industrial centers. Today these modes of life are rapidly being eroded as capitalism finalizes the colonization of older enclaves. As theorists of capitalist modernity—from Max Weber to Karl Polanyi—argued, such "completion" of modernity under capitalism may sound its death knell. Those theses were sketchy and perhaps premature when they were formulated. Today, they may well be coming into their own, which is one of the reasons I have embarked on this book, as I did on the sailboat.

With my Italian sailor friends, we traded stories and jokes, as seamen are wont to do. It also helped for my thought process that two of the fellow seafarers were a seasoned diplomat and a seasoned social scientist. Each of them had moved into the ranks of the "emeritocracy in their respective professions." As we approached the coast of Sicily, I was struck by one story in particular. It was a legend from the two largest islands of Italy: Sardinia and Sicily.

Over the centuries the two islands were ravaged by invasions of all kinds: Saracens and Crusaders, pirates and papists, and many others too. The villagers protected themselves by leaving the coasts and running for the hills where a peculiar culture of diffidence—(the famous *omertà*)—emerged. Even today, these are people of few words, for fear of denunciation and retaliation. One of their traditions has persisted and is still passed along *sotto voce*. American scholars have called this Southern culture "amoral familism."[4] It can be summed up thus: for our family everything; for everybody else silence and suspicion.

In the old days, when a family member—usually one who is very old—declined in health and entered a state of prolonged agony, the relatives would convene, and, with few words and solemn gestures, decide to put the ailing loved one out of his or her misery. They knew it was time "to summon her."

She was referred to as *la accabadora*, the midwife of the moribund. She came with a wooden hammer. She was left alone with the dying person. Then quickly and expertly she applied a precise blow to the back of the cranium, and the patient was gone. The priest, who had already been called, administered the viaticum and the holy oils. Now the wailing could begin, the goods of the departed could be distributed, and the wake proceeded until the procession moved through the village and the corpse was laid to rest when the final prayer was said.

Acabar in Spanish means to finish (in sexual parlance it also means "to come," and consummation is thought of as a "little death"). In Sardinian dialect, *accabadora* is the lady who brings something or somebody to its end. In the eyes of the community, she is not a murderer but a person who, with love and piety, helps destiny accomplish its "telos." She is in a way the "ultimate mother"—a terrible mother, like the mothers in Federico García Lorca's poem of death.[5]

In the military, to shorten the agony of a man condemned to death but poorly executed, an officer was called upon to apply the merciful *coup de grâce*. The civilian equivalent still exists in this old Sardinian custom—now largely gone—in which the *accabadora* was called to the deathbed of a patient to finish him or her off.

The legend is now better known thanks to Michela Murgia's successful novel with the title *La Accabadora*.[6] In the story, one of the main characters, Bonaria Urrai, is the *accabadora* of the area; she portrays an angel of mercy who tends to the chronically sick and dying, acting as a kind of interceder between life here below and the great beyond. In other words, she practices euthanasia. I find this story an apt metaphor for the politics of our days. I will examine a few cases.

Willingly or not, a number of Western politicians, driven by an angry populace, are now playing this terminal role. Despite attempts to exonerate Europe with ever-weaker arguments, it looks like a never-ending agony in light of the struggles to replace the Union with a revival of nations, the wrath of voting populations, and the rise to prominence of demagogues. Little surprise then to witness these actions seeking to call the whole thing off. But what will follow this new and enigmatic Finnegan's wake?

Like *accabadoras*, a number of politicians, driven by an angry populace, are now posing as midwives of the moribund. The English referendum favoring Brexit is one more spasm in the long agony of the European Union. An inept prime minister made the fatal mistake of calling for a vote, and was hoisted with his own petard, as Shakespeare would say. Those who voted "Leave" acted as the *accabadors*. What is not clear yet is whether their blow was decisive enough. But if not, other *accabadors* may finish the job—nationalist pied pipers like Mr. Nigel Farage, who will be telling their followers that no rat should stay in a sinking ship. But cold water awaits them, and the question becomes, do they know how to swim in their fantasized post-global world?

There have been other such attempts before, as with the Greek bid to secede under then Prime Minister Papandreou (he was forced to resign), which was followed by a semi-coma imposed with the help of a financial respirator. Later on, when a leftist party came to power, the colorful Greek finance minister Yanis Varoufakis was not allowed to stay with the "adults" in the so-called European family room for fear that he too might become an unwanted *accabador*. His original party *Syriza* finally submitted to the interminable discipline imposed from the outside by Germany and other wardens.

As for other "weaker" members of the Union—like Spain, they are condemned to preside over the sacrifice of an entire generation that will soon cease to be young. Meanwhile, Spain cannot be governed well, and new forces like *Podemos* will still carry the hammer of the *accabadora*. In England, for example, the murderous midwives were largely old; in the case of Spain they are mostly young.

Of the healthier "core" European economies, Holland is tempted to secede as well. Geert Wilders, the right-wing populist, is an *accabador*-in-waiting for the Dutch. A domino effect is underway as the European Union fades into the past like a distant dream: a sort of utopia for tired men that has been "dreamed out." The German philosopher Edmund Husserl put it even better when he spoke of Western culture, in a tone of desperation: *"Der Traum ist ausgeträumt"* ("The dream is over").[7]

After Brexit, what's Nexit? The anger at the global elite has exploded here and there, and everywhere else, continues to seethe, while the people's spleen (mostly older working people) has been expressed. British politicians join the pack to stay in power and then try to backpedal. They feel like Christian Scientists with appendicitis.

The Eurocrats in Brussels are frantically doing what they do best: convening emergency meetings that result in tepid banalities. They are hatching new bureaucratic maneuvers. Those on the deck of the *Titanic* at least were having fun dancing their way toward the invisible iceberg. The joyless Eurocrats, however, chitchat about the visible peril but are unable to act, in extremis as well as in other, more ignorable crises—as when they sacked those Greek politicians who dared call a referendum. Democracy has never been the strong suit of Eurocrats. To them C.P. Cavafy's poem "Waiting for the Barbarians" sadly applies:

> What are we waiting for, assembled in the forum?
> The barbarians are due here today.
> Why isn't anything happening in the senate?

> Why do the senators sit there without legislating?
> Because the barbarians are coming today.
> What laws can the senators make now?
> Once the barbarians are here, they'll do the legislating.
> Why did our emperor get up so early,
> and why is he sitting at the city's main gate
> on his throne, in state, wearing the crown?
> Because the barbarians are coming today
> and the emperor is waiting to receive their leader.
> He has even prepared a scroll to give him,
> replete with titles, with imposing names.
> Why have our two consuls and praetors come out today
> wearing their embroidered, their scarlet togas?
> Why have they put on bracelets with so many amethysts,
> and rings sparkling with magnificent emeralds?
> Why are they carrying elegant canes
> beautifully worked in silver and gold?
> Because the barbarians are coming today
> and things like that dazzle the barbarians.
> Why don't our distinguished orators come forward as usual
> to make their speeches, say what they have to say?
> Because the barbarians are coming today
> and they're bored by rhetoric and public speaking.
> Why this sudden restlessness, this confusion?
> (How serious people's faces have become.)
> Why are the streets and squares emptying so rapidly,
> everyone going home so lost in thought?
> Because night has fallen and the barbarians have not come.
> And some who have just returned from the border say
> there are no barbarians any longer.
> And now, what's going to happen to us without barbarians?
> They were, those people, a kind of solution.[8]

What about the Italians? Soon the Italians too may bolt, perhaps even re-adopt the lira, and thus become all millionaires in devalued currency and quasi-defaulted debt, as in yesteryear.[9] For Italians, the comedian-actor Beppe Grillo may play the role of *accabador*, especially after Matteo Renzi, the former prime minister, in calling a referendum on reform (which was a referendum on his government), made a bet as bad as David Cameron's in the UK, and like Cameron, lost.

What will the French do? Under President François Hollande they followed more or less the Germans. But with the rise of Marine Le Pen, or with their own exit referendum, they could have followed the example of those Le Pen called the "brave" English? That would have given the world the strange spectacle of two historic rivals joining in the same suicidal mission, disguised as a courageous jump over the trenches, as in the First World War. The election of Emanuel Macron was a moment of sobriety in a nation prone to excess. It allowed France to evade the fate of the UK, but the situation remains fragile.

This litany leaves us to consider the center pivot of the EU: a powerful nation that initially benefitted from the euro by merrily sponsoring debt among the lesser members so they could buy its products. When the giddy dance of debt stopped and the clients went broke, their Teutonic master imposed austerity on them, telling them to become "like us" and not to "burden us" with bailouts from the profligacy "we" once endorsed. Now Germany stands alone: a European superpower too big for the continent and too small for the world, guided by a school marm who nonetheless is the only statesperson of stature in Europe. Their markets in Europe are running dry; their austerity recipes are unviable and unenviable. Germany has become a reluctant and isolated liberal Reich in a Europe that cannot and does not want to be a German Europe any more. Eventually, it too might "exit" either by a Germanic triumph of the will or more meekly by letting the rest disintegrate. It will have, as in the past, to look east for an accommodation with the Russian "near abroad"—the Eastern European countries that were once satellites of the Soviet Union—and with Russia itself. Merkel one day will be gone and new leaders, right or left, may emerge.

The specter of fragmentation is for the moment held in abeyance, but Europe still waits for the barbarians. In the end a new fragmented Europe may consist of pettier nationalisms, immigration barriers (their version of Trump walls), local (devalued) currencies as a means to enact more elegant defaults under a different name, and a beggar-thy-neighbor set of economic policies. "Win-win" negotiations could then be replaced by "lose-lose" deals. What else can follow the hour of the *accabadors*?

What a terrible geopolitical distraction at a historic turning point! If Brexit was, in the end, a tremor in Europe, the election of Donald Trump in America was an earthquake of greater magnitude. In its aftermath, Americans are caught in a mounting fight between authoritarian nationalists in a disorderly Washington with a base in the geographical center of the country, and increasingly intransigent resisters on the coasts. The Europeans fret, and the Chinese smile inscrutably from afar. But the axis of world history inexorably moves east.

Over the years, many cherished American institutions have been hollowed out. The bipartisan system got entangled in a gridlock, which affected governance and produced a vacuum at the top. This in turn created the opportunity for an outsider to occupy that top. The upshot is that politics has become divisive inside each party, paralyzed between parties, authoritarian at the executive level, and extra-parliamentary in opposition, which—without traditional party channels—has moved to the streets. Historically, the phenomenon is not unprecedented, except this time it is fueled by the electronic social media.[10]

The transition from Obama's weak administration to Trump's unstable congregation went beyond a change of government. It was a change of regime. The new regime seems to be both pugnacious to the point of being undemocratic, and disorganized. Many Trump supporters celebrate his advent as a return to an imagined community—white, homogeneous, Christian—which they no longer recognize in the global, multicultural, high-tech present, and wish to restore.

The paradoxes abound. Working-class anger gave support to a government staffed by plutocrats, not precisely worker-friendly. Protection policies result in a hollow mercantilism. Trump trumpets industrial policies without the industry. Mexicans and Chinese are blamed for the replacement of jobs—by robots. The retreat from multilateral treatises accelerates the global rise of China. The list of paradoxes, unintended consequences, and sheer contradictions is long.

The heralded rapprochement with Russia (derailed as of this writing) may have benefits in the fight against international terrorism,[11] although the United States would be forced to share the prize, and the price in prestige. America would no longer set the agenda. The new American president's statement that NATO is "obsolete" contained a grain of truth, but not the whole truth. By the same token, it signaled the obsolescence of the American-designed post-Second World War order. In the past, what was good for the goose (the United States) was good for the gander (Europe). Today, what is bad for the gander (EU) is bad for the goose (United States) as well. As they said in the sixteenth century, "as deepe drinketh the Goose as the Gander"—but this time, the drink will be vodka. And there are new geese in the flock. Russia is rising; China is rising.

The American rivalry with China is not going too well for Washington. As the United States remains largely distracted by domestic tensions and protracted wars, China has moved vigorously to enact an agenda of its own style of globalization without the usual Western-oriented liberal strictures. China is a firm believer in the hard tools of power, and agnostic about the soft. This is clear in its endorsement of trade liberalization, the establishment of the Asian Infrastructure Investment Bank to both complement and compete with US-designed older multilateral agencies, and the "One Belt, One Road" initiative to improve connections with Europe and the rest of Asia—a veritable new Silk Road.[12]

In relation to Russia, American policy makers and pundits have often remarked that a declining nuclear-armed former superpower can cause a lot of harm. In reference to the United States, I would add: *de te fabula narratur*—that a declining former single superpower can also cause a lot of harm if it does not adjust to a new reality of great-power relations that it cannot dominate any more. Under the Trump administration the United States seems to have adopted a posture of belligerent retrenchment.[13]

The evidence I have gathered from experts and journalists in different countries, as I was researching this book, suggests that having interfered in the American electoral process (although both the scope of the interference and its effectiveness are under ongoing investigation) and having placed a good bet on the behavior of American voters, Russia attained a strategic objective. Contrary to what many people think, the objective was not to have a friendlier and reliable partner in the American administration but rather to have, in Washington, a chaotic and incompetent rival. If this is true, then the risk of armed conflict is greater, not lesser, than in the past.

The 45th American president is riding a sort of wave of popular reaction that is a concoction of legitimate grievances, nostalgia, and scapegoating. The situation is not unique to America. The specter of popular reaction runs through the entire Western world. What will the president—a foul-mouthed billionaire who entertains the populace with a festival of scandals and witch-hunts, while he gives to the rich and privileged large gifts—deliver for his electoral base except rhetorical sops?[14] Many months after his election, I can testify that the atmosphere is anxious and tense.

In such atmosphere—the despondency of some, the defiance of others, and the vengeful celebration of many—my annual pilgrimage to Italy at year's end provided a reprieve from the crossfire and an opportunity to remember and reflect.

I will spare the reader, in these pages, one more comparison between President Donald Trump and the several-times Prime Minister of Italy Silvio Berlusconi. Others have done so already, and mostly on the level of anecdote. For those interested in a serious exercise along these lines, I recommend one book: Maurizio Viroli's *The Liberty of Servants: Berlusconi's Italy*.[15] During my Italian tour, more distant and strategic visions occupied my mind. The United States is not Italy. Issues in America have an immediate global impact, rising well above the anecdotal, the folkloric, and the parochial-American bent toward identity politics and a sometimes-ferocious *Kulturkampf*. Here we are dealing with raw global power that is *geo*-politics.[16] Therefore, a more apt comparison is with ancient Rome.

Back to Paestum as a site of hypothetical reflections: in January its solitude (there were no tourist crowds) gave me the sensation of a haunted place, full of echoes from past chores and the muted voices of the dead. My feet stepped on the remnants of the Greek *agora* and the Roman *forum*, places where ancient citizens used to meet and make deals, among them an exchange of ideas under the guidance of *Mens Bona*. And I recalled how this came to an end, in stages first, and then abruptly, until those early imperfect versions of a government of the people, by the people, for the people vanished from the Earth.

Empires decay invisibly for a long time, until the stress becomes apparent and at times spectacular, which allows posterity to fix a date for the demise. Only a few empires come to a sudden end—such as the defeat of the Third Reich in the Second World War or the televised moment when Mr. Gorbachev "closed the book" on the Soviet empire. But Rome was different. As the saying goes, it was not built in a day—nor did it end in one day either. That day came after a long process of societal and political decay, entwined in its very power and expansion, and while its system sowed the world with fertile seeds of culture and civilization. The story is told and explained in a very large array of books—not always in accordance with each other—that can easily fill a library.

Along such process of defeasance, Julius Caesar took a decisive step on January 10, 49 BCE (exactly 2,066 years before my visit to the ruins of Paestum). Faced with prosecution for war crimes, Caesar had to submit or rebel. On that date, he chose to defy the Republic and advance on Rome, at the head of his troops. In their superstitions, Romans thought that certain rivers should not be crossed, like the fabled *Rio del Olvido* in Galicia, Spain,[17] and they thought the same about Rubicon, the river that runs from the Apennine Mountains to the Adriatic Sea. Caesar crossed that river and history changed.

Caesar's defiance, and the ensuing civil war, did not bode well for the Republic. The latter was an oligarchy that rested on what Max Weber called "competitive elitism" (proto-democracy), with one faction leaning on the popular Assembly and the other on the aristocratic Senate. Caesar abolished this two-party game, while assuming the mantle of one of them: the *populares*. In fact, many of Caesar's measures indeed seemed to protect the ordinary people against the selfish policy of the nobles of the establishment, but he did this as a way to establish a strong base for a personal regime. His trick was clever, and successful: extending citizenship to the "forgotten outsiders"—those who had fought for Rome but did not enjoy its privileges. Ever since then, *Caesarism* is a name used to characterize authoritarian populism.[18] I think the parallel with the present day is clear.[19]

Julius Caesar's dictatorship was short lived. Faced with the prospect of tyranny, the Roman senators used the only resort they thought appropriate to temper it—tyrannicide. But the harm was done. Far from returning to the republican balance of power, Rome plunged once more into civil war until Octavianus (Caesar's designated heir and adopted son), having vanquished his rivals, assumed total power as Emperor Augustus and inaugurated the famed *pax romana*. The Republic was never officially disavowed. Augustus was a consummate PR man. The magistrates became legally and practically subservient to one citizen with power over all. Republican institutions were kept, but only as a façade. They had become empty shells.

The imperial regime was brittle though. Despite the Augustan peace, it was frequently challenged from without and from within. The succession of power holders was extremely irregular. Rome was a fitful empire. Of the 85 emperors in Roman history, only five were reputedly good ones—with Marcus Aurelius standing above the rest. Yet, no fewer than 17 were assassinated. Rome experienced imperial overreach and internal corruption. It declined and disappeared as the world's greatest power. It left behind a spectacular legacy to which many pay homage today.

Back from the ruins, in Trump's America, I felt it merited posing again a question that has been posed before, but now seemed more poignant: are we Rome?[20] To answer this question, we must take a retrospective look at what had been brewing silently until it broke out in full daylight in the societies of the West, with consequences that might be dire—but are still unknown. What happens in America is not a singular aberration: it is part of a trend. Large swaths of the population in different Western countries, in their anger at being left behind, want "to shake things up" in the hope that the reshuffle will deal them a better hand. They expect outsiders to deliver them from current establishments, and thus, bring to an end what looks more and more like an *Ancien Régime*.

In what is perhaps the finest historical novel written by an American, John Williams imagined a letter that Julius Caesar wrote in 44 BCE to Octavius, his adopted son:

> ...How long have we been living the Roman lie? Ever since I can remember, certainly; perhaps for many years before. And from what source does that lie suck its energy, so that it grows stronger than the truth? We have seen murder, theft, and

pillage in the name of the Republic –and call it the necessary price we pay for freedom. Cicero deplores the depraved Roman morality that worships wealth –and himself a millionaire many times over, travels with a hundred slaves from one of his villas to another. A consul speaks of peace and tranquility –and raises armies that will murder the colleague whose power threatens his self-interest. The Senate speaks of freedom –and thrusts upon me powers that I do not want but must accept and use if Rome is to endure. Is there no answer to the lie?

I have conquered the world, and none of it is secure, I have shown plenty liberty to the people, and they flee it as if it were a disease, I despise those whom I can trust, and love those best who would quickly betray me. And I do not know where we are going, though I lead a nation to its destiny.[21]

In the same political-fiction vein, I can well imagine a similar letter written by Dwight Eisenhower to George Kennan in the past, or by an American *accabador* to a disciple in the present. And so I ask again: are we Rome?

Notes

1 See Ronald Syme, *The Roman Revolution* (New York: Oxford University Press, 1939).
2 Curzio Malaparte, *Coup d'État: The Technique of Revolution* (New York: Dutton, 1932); Edward N. Luttwak, *Coup d'Etat: A Practical Handbook*, revised ed. (Cambridge, MA: Harvard University Press, 2016).
3 Corradi, *The Fitful Republic* (Boulder, CO: Westview Press, 1985).
4 Edward Banfield, *The Moral Basis of a Backward Society* (Glencoe, IL: Free Press, 1958). In a study of Montegrano, Italy, Banfield observed "the inability of the villagers to act together for their common good or, indeed, for any end transcending the immediate, material interest of the nuclear family."
5 Federico García Lorca, *Lament for the Death of a Bullfighter and Other Poems*, trans. A.L. Lloyd (1937, repr., London: Faber & Faber, 2008). www.boppin.com/lorca/lament.html.
  "*No se cerraron sus ojos cuando vio los cuernos cerca, pero las madres terrible levantaron la cabeza.*"
  (His eyes did not close when he saw the horns near, but the terrible mothers lifted their heads.)

6. Michela Murgia, *La Accabadora* (Torino, Italy: Luigi Einaudi, 2009).
7. Edmund Husserl, *The Crisis of European Science and Transcendental Phenomenology* (Evanston, IL: Northwestern University Press, 1970), 389.
8. C.P. Cavafy, *Collected Poems*, ed. George Savidis, trans. Edmund Keeley and Philip Sherrard, revised ed. (Princeton, NJ: Princeton University Press, 1992).
9. For an analysis of possible scenarios, see Wolfgang Münchau, "Italy May Be the Next Domino to Fall," *Financial Times*, June 26, 2016.
10. The precedents are presented in Elias Canetti's *Crowds and Power*, which, together with other remarkable texts, won him the Nobel Prize (for literature, since there has never been such prize for social science, and economics had not yet joined the fry).
11. See the proposal by Luis Moreno Ocampo, "How Trump Can Work with Russia to Challenge the Status Quo and to Control ISIS," *Just Security*, January 18, 2017, www.justsecurity.org/36449/trump-work-russia-challenge-status-quo-control-isis/.
12. On the global financial stage, it is worth noticing the shift in the balance of so-called swap lines between central banks. Traditionally, they are fund lines that the US Federal Reserve maintains with its overseas counterparts to make dollars (the international reserve currency) available in case of stress. But these swap lines are only with Japan, the EU, the UK, Switzerland, and Canada. The People's Bank of China, in contrast to the five swap lines from the Fed, maintains 37. The weight of global finance is moving east, and helping the global south.
13. "Situation Report: South China Sea: U.S. Will Defend International Territories from China, White House Says," *Stratfor Worldview*, January 24, 2017, https://worldview.stratfor.com/situation-report/south-china-sea-us-will-defend-international-territories-china-white-house-says. This is the Rand Corporation analysis: David C. Gompert *et al.*, "War with China: Thinking through the Unthinkable," Rand Corporation, 2016, www.rand.org/content/dam/rand/pubs/research_reports/RR1100/RR1140/RAND_RR1140.pdf.
14. With a favorable tax policy for corporations and the rich, cash may return to the United States, but it is likely to fuel more mergers and acquisitions than the creation of jobs. Manufacturing employment is likely to fall, not rise. The repeal of the Affordable Care Act will leave millions without coverage. This is hardly a recipe for sustained support, unless international tensions feed a zeal for war abroad and repression at home.

15 Maurizio Viroli, *The Liberty of Servants. Berlusconi's Italy* (Princeton, NJ: Princeton University Press, 2011).
16 The concept of soft power has, in my view, run its course as a prolonged academic oxymoron. Today, it would seem that Carl Schmitt is more relevant than Joseph Nye.
17 Legend has it that after crossing the river, you no longer remember who you are.
18 Franz Neumann, "Notes on the Theory of Dictatorship," in *The Democratic and the Authoritarian State* (Glencoe, IL: Free Press, 1957).
19 Witness Donald Trump's oratory in favor of the *populares*: "For too long, a small group in our nation's capital has reaped the rewards of government while the people have borne the cost. Washington flourished, but the people did not share in its wealth. Politicians prospered, but the jobs left. [...] The forgotten men and women of our country will be forgotten no longer" (from Donald Trump's inaugural address, January 20, 2017).
20 For a parallel treatment, see Cullen Murphy, *Are We Rome? The Fall of an Empire and the Fate of America* (New York: Houghton Mifflin, 2007).
21 John Williams, *Augustus* (1972, repr., New York: The New York Review of Books Classics, 2014), 18–19.

References

Banfield, Edward. *The Moral Basis of a Backward Society* (Glencoe, IL: Free Press, 1958).
Canetti, Elias. *Crowds and Power* (New York: Farrar, Strauss and Giroux, 1984).
Cavafy, C.P. *Collected Poems*, ed. George Savidis, trans. Edmund Keeley and Philip Sherrard, revised ed. (Princeton, NJ: Princeton University Press, 1992).
Corradi, Juan E. *The Fitful Republic* (Boulder, CO: Westview Press, 1985).
Gompert, David C. *et al.* "War with China: Thinking through the Unthinkable," Rand Corporation, 2016, www.rand.org/content/dam/rand/pubs/research_reports/RR1100/RR1140/RAND_RR1140.pdf.
Husserl, Edmund. *The Crisis of European Science and Transcendental Phenomenology* (Evanston, IL: Northwestern University Press, 1970).
Lorca, Federico García. *Lament for the Death of a Bullfighter and Other Poems*, trans. A.L. Lloyd (1937, repr., London: Faber & Faber, 2008).
Luttwak, Edward N. *Coup d'Etat: A Practical Handbook*, revised ed. (Cambridge, MA: Harvard University Press, 2016).
Malaparte, Curzio. *Coup d'État: The Technique of Revolution* (New York: Dutton, 1932).

Münchau, Wolfgang. "Italy May Be the Next Domino to Fall," *Financial Times*, June 26, 2016.

Murgia, Michela. *La Accabadora* (Torino, Italy: Luigi Einaudi, 2009).

Murphy, Cullen. *Are We Rome? The Fall of an Empire and the Fate of America* (New York: Houghton Mifflin, 2007).

Neumann, Franz. "Notes on the Theory of Dictatorship," in *The Democratic and the Authoritarian State* (Glencoe, IL: Free Press, 1957).

Ocampo, Luis Moreno. "How Trump Can Work with Russia to Challenge the Status Quo and to Control ISIS," *Just Security*, January 18, 2017, www.justsecurity.org/36449/trump-work-russia-challenge-status-quo-control-isis/.

"Situation Report: South China Sea: U.S. Will Defend International Territories from China, White House Says," *Stratfor Worldview*, January 24, 2017, https://worldview.stratfor.com/situation-report/south-china-sea-us-will-defend-international-territories-china-white-house-says.

Syme, Ronald. *The Roman Revolution* (New York: Oxford University Press, 1939).

Trump, Donald J. *Inaugural Address*, January 20, 2017.

Viroli, Maurizio Viroli. *The Liberty of Servants. Berlusconi's Italy* (Princeton, NJ: Princeton University Press, 2011).

Williams, John. *Augustus* (1972, repr., New York: The New York Review of Books Classics, 2014).

7

BEHEMOTH LITE

*National–Populist Democracy and
Its Impact on Strategy*

The current wave of right-wing populism in the West is a far cry from historical and progressive populisms in the developing world. It is narrow-minded, reactionary, persecutory, and oblivious to the consequences. This chapter explores the geopolitical consequences of the trend. The conclusion: what succeeds inside does not work outside, and a disorderly foreign policy on the part of major powers is likely to ensue.

What are the factors that contribute to strategic mistakes in power politics, and especially in the foreign interventions of a world power? In this chapter, I shall review some of those factors. It is apt to start with an analogy from seamanship, since geopolitical strategy is after all, the art of steering the ship of state.

In detailed inspections of accidents of vessels at sea as well as accidents of aviation, a chain of events (or error chain) refers to the many contributing factors that lead to a crash rather than one single event.[1] These contributing actions typically stem from human factor-related mistakes—such as a captain's (or pilot's) error—rather than mechanical failure. In the international arena, the behavior of states is seriously affected by the dynamics of their internal political processes, and sometimes such internal dynamics produce a chain of strategic errors in the geopolitical domain. For example, the fear of a terrorist attack, as in other moral panics, may be way out of proportion to the real statistical risks.[2] But neither rational discourse nor publicized facts will assuage such fears among the populace. A political leader may then stoke fears in order to energize his or her political base and give a focus to their general anxiety. Actions taken to protect the population under such circumstances may be deleterious to actual security in the real world.

In a celebrated lecture on politics as a vocation,[3] Max Weber referred to an emerging possibility in modern polities that he called "plebiscitary leader democracy" (*plebiszitären Führerdemokratie*).[4] As a German nationalist but an objective and a lucid analyst as well, Weber did not dismiss that formula because he thought that charismatic leadership might provide a balance to the soulless and impersonal machinery of modern government, and thus bridge the distance between the public and state institutions.

Political judgment in the complex modern world is a challenge even to the most skillful statesman or stateswoman. Such judgment, Weber contended, is learned through the actual exercise of political power. It has to be honed by practical political education—that is, through long experience of formulating intentions and assessing their possible outcomes. Adherence to a coherent and stable set of ends and to instrumental reasoning (*Zweckrationalität*) toward those ends requires a form of objectivity, an aplomb that has to be learned. This is genuine strategic vision. Weber called it "the politics of responsibility."

Weber insisted that in the absence of such a political education,[5] if lay people are entrusted to make political decisions or judge political outcomes, they are liable to respond emotionally. For Weber, the aggregation of their fitful whims and desires can be a dangerously destabilizing political force. A responsible leader, aided by a dose of charisma, knows how to steer those emotions while keeping a cool head when making decisions and understand their likely consequences.[6]

One could add to these Weberian strictures that even calculated positions on an issue deemed urgent or important by the populace (*Wertrationalität*) produce poor governance if that issue is isolated from other issues. For instance, a referendum is a direct vote in which an entire electorate is asked to vote on a particular proposal. This may result in the adoption of a new law, but it is seldom part of a comprehensive strategic vision.

But what happens when the leaders themselves are charismatic but ignorant, irrational and unprepared; when, in leading, they follow simplistic and stubborn beliefs regardless of consequences; or worse yet, when they are just corrupt? In this case, the destabilization is compounded. In societies that have grown very unequal, conflictive, and resentful, there may be a hidden—even unconscious—*raison d'être* asserting itself behind the irrationality. Irrationality produces, on occasion, high political payoffs.

Democracy is fragile, and cannot survive without daily and informed practice. Many Americans, after centuries of regular elections, have grown complacent with a democracy deemed automatic while the polarization of their main political parties has grown to such an extent that governance is frequently stalled. An opposition party used to devoting all its efforts to blocking the initiatives of the party in power cannot hone its skills in dealing with serious domestic and geostrategic challenges. When it is its own turn to govern, it simply enacts measures to satisfy pet ideological projects and, in the absence of a restraining strategic vision, is prone to just enrich its members and sponsors in rapacious and destructive ways. Meanwhile, among sectors of the underlying population the yearning for an outside "savior" grows. There is then a combination of extreme partisanship with authoritarian arbitration.

Sometimes, the main threat to a political system is not just an extreme or narrow ideology but also a chaotic execution of it. *Autoritarismus gemildert durch Schlumperei* (authoritarianism tempered by incompetence) is an old German expression that gives hope to those who believe that sheer sloppiness and confusion may limit autocracy. And yet there is method to the madness. For example, when, in a constitutional republic, the executive branch issues an impulsive decree to close borders in order "to protect the nation"—even though there is no evidence of clear and present danger, the courts (the judicial branch) may challenge the diktat. In rejecting the court's arguments, such an executive may set a course toward constitutional confrontation. The executive will be much criticized and eventually lose the fight, or be forced to backtrack. In the short run, the outcome will be celebrated as a triumph of the balance of power that is enshrined in the constitution. But this will occlude an underlying strategy that seems to come straight out of Machiavelli's playbook: by losing to the courts the executive branch is insulated from criticism if and when a terrorist attack takes place, and will allow the executive to deflect blame away from himself and put it on the courts and the bureaucracy, claiming "I told you so." This is how an autocracy is built.

According to the great-yet-infamous German political theorist Carl Schmitt, the existence of exceptional situations (real or manufactured) "refutes the formal face of legal liberalism, which argues that pre-established legal norms cover and apply to all possible situations."[7] The need to take immediate action in an emergency strengthens the role of the executive who must decide how to deal with the emergency on an ad-hoc basis. The gates are open to a case-by-case decisionism.

In such eventuality, an administration is less a "normal" government than a small clique (or set of cliques) that is not well connected to the very people (the bureaucrats, for example) who help them get things done, but is constantly disrupting their routines. There is such a thing as rule by confusion.

In his mild praise of charismatic leadership, Weber did not foresee the national-socialist Behemoth lurking in his country under the Weimar Republic.[8] Others thought otherwise. Years later, reflecting upon his political achievements, Joseph Goebbels stated, "This will always remain one of the best jokes of democracy, that it gave its deadly enemies the means by which it was destroyed."[9] After the demise of the Weimar Republic, it took time and effort for social scientists to understand how the Nazi organization of society involved the collapse of traditional ideas of the state, of ideology, of law, and even of any underlying rationality.

Franz Neumann's study of the theory and practice of National Socialism attempted to show that behind the authoritarian and autocratic façade of the regime, there was ultimately nothing but terror, egotism, and arbitrariness on the part of certain social groups that had seized different levers of control. Sometimes the concentration of power—even when it is distributed among a few cliques at the top, but without the mediation of institutions—is achieved by provoking chaos. Cola Di Rienzo, Savonarola, Hitler, Stalin, and Mao were masters in the dark arts of disruption and confusion. In 2017, an updated version of this mode of behavior is exemplified by the words of White House former Chief Strategist, Stephen Bannon. Giving rare public remarks, he said that the Trump cabinet was working toward the "deconstruction of the administrative state."[10]

As the world careens toward reactionary populism and voters, at times, succeed in electing authoritarian demagogues to the highest offices in their lands, it behooves us to assess the impact of these new regimes—"Behemoth lite"—on geopolitics.

On the paths through which populists accede to power, it is worth noticing that instead of relying primarily on new parties, populists have either infiltrated or taken over traditional conservative parties (in the UK and the United States)—as argued by Jan-Werner Müller.[11] This raises an important question. What induces groups to surrender power and to legitimate this surrender? In his book, *Ruling Oneself Out*,[12] Ivan Ermakoff focuses on two paradigmatic cases of such surrender—the passing of an enabling bill granting Hitler the right to amend the Weimar constitution without parliamentary supervision (1933) and the transfer of full executive, legislative, and constitutional powers to Marshal Petain in Vichy France (1940). Ermakoff recasts abdications as the outcome of a process of collective alignment that, in my estimate, has been happening in the United States and the UK for quite some time, and in several other important countries as well. Here, I shall consider only the geopolitical consequences *after* the abdication happens.

When pondering the various foreign policies that often result from a new national-populist dispensation, it is hard to discern a coherent strategy. That is because what may succeed inside does not work outside. Rule by confusion may strengthen the hands of national-populists at home but is deleterious to any world order. At best, such policies lead to new volatile situations. Foreign policy "old hands," like Zbigniew Brzezinski, foretold it and warned us of the dangers.[13] Why such a sobering conclusion?

With all its pros and cons, globalization has made the world more interdependent than it ever was. The unprecedented compression of space and time, in markets, interpersonal communications, technological development and diffusion, mass migrations, and the rapid impact of all these on climate and the environment, today forms a multidimensional sociological web that is much denser than the Internet. As a consequence, a strategic vision requires knowing and connecting these dimensions, and proposes a path that favors the best advantages globalization affords humanity, mitigating its various dysfunctions.

But populism and its twin, nationalism, do not connect the dots.[14] Through their leaders, they are prone instead to exploit a series of disjointed single issues. A single-issue focus distracts the public with multiple discrete solicitations and prevents the individual from developing an ecological view that deals with complexity.[15] Unconnected initiatives—often no more specific than slogans and impulsive proclamations—are checked off either serially or simultaneously, without formulating the linkages among them or anticipating second-order effects, and (to use the old language of sociology) their likely latent functions.[16]

In the international arena, national-populism is a way to make nations individually stronger but in appearance only,[17] with pageantry and bombast rather than substance, and in the case of superpowers, also over-stretched. As a result, the risks of war increase, or more precisely, multiply.[18] Case-by-case decisionism at home facilitates chains of errors abroad.[19] Here are a few examples.

As nations wish to guard their interests in trade and security, they can either pursue the path of organizing alliances and trade pacts (today, more likely regional than global) or choose to "get tough"—that is, turn their backs on each other. The latter is a lose-lose situation. In Pareto's terminology,[20] the geopolitical situation calls for the cunning of foxes, not the roaring of lions. Under national-populism, nations will get the exact opposite—the wrong posture at the wrong time. In the words of the *conservative* head of the German parliament,

> Whoever champions a closed mind instead of openness to the world, whoever literally walls themselves [sic] in, bets on protectionism instead of free trade and preaches isolationism instead of states cooperating, and declares 'We first' as a program, should not be surprised if others do the same—with all the fatal side effects for international ties which we know from the 20th century.[21]

Closing borders in thoughtless ways may be popular as a reassertion of "sovereignty," but the likely consequences of such an action are the disruption of supply chains, higher prices for national consumers, and higher labor costs—which, given the dynamics of capitalism, will lead to the faster replacement of workers by robots. To cite the successful investor Seth Klarman, "While they might be popular, the reason the U.S. long ago abandoned protectionist trade policies is because they not only don't work, they actually leave society worse off."[22]

Although China is still much less powerful than the United States, its economic size and ambition combined with population size make it the only potential other superpower. Its further rise is inevitable (barring total war). Until now, many people in the West were concerned that in its rise China would retain an authoritarian and illiberal political system instead of following the example of the West—although they were hopeful that in the end Western liberal lessons would prevail. But as the West moves in a pronounced authoritarian direction itself, and its much-heralded "soft power" dissipates, China's counterbalancing prestige as a pragmatic "can-do" power will increase.

In the Pacific, China's regional heft will increase as a result of the precipitous American withdrawal from the Trans Pacific Partnership (TPP) in 2017. Republican Senator John McCain described the president's decision as a,

> serious mistake that will have lasting consequences for America's economy and our strategic position in the Asia-Pacific region. It will create an opening for China to rewrite the economic rules of the road at the expense of American workers. And it will send a troubling signal of American disengagement in the Asia-Pacific region at a time we can least afford it.

China-led institutions have proved appealing to a growing number of countries. Most US allies have joined the Asian Infrastructure Investment Bank, despite American opposition.

Strategically, China's patient attitude toward Trumpian bombast follows an old geopolitical rule—valid from General Sun Tzu's *The Art of War* to the present—and best expressed by Napoleon Bonaparte:

"Never interrupt your enemy when he is making a mistake."[23] Moreover, recently the Chinese power elite has joined Russia and other powers at the gambling table of high-stakes corruption—another weapon in the quest to shape American strategic decisions. It has granted concessionary permits to the for-profit organization of the president of the United States.

Trump's triumph in the fight to wrest back his brand for construction services could prove to be the first of many intellectual property victories in China during his presidency. Each win creates value for Trump's business empire, and ethics questions about his administration.[24]

Some countries could use Trump's desire to consolidate control over his brand to extend—or withhold—favor, especially in a place such as China where the courts and bureaucracy are influenced by the ruling Communist Party and, by design, reflect the leadership's political imperatives. While China recently has shown greater interest in protecting intellectual property rights in general, simply the possibility that the country could use trademarks as leverage has drawn concern.

Russia has pioneered the deployment of business deals—Russian style—as a foreign policy weapon. The Putin regime is not interested in just cozy relations with Washington. Its strategic objectives have been attained in its helping to establish an American administration that is permeable to infiltration at the highest levels. As reported in *The New Yorker*:

> Alexey Venediktov, the editor-in-chief of *Echo of Moscow*, and a figure with deep contacts inside the Russian political élite, said, "Trump was attractive to people in Russia's political establishment as a disturber of the peace for their counterparts in the American political establishment." Venediktov suggested that, for Putin and those closest to him, any support that the Russian state provided to Trump's candidacy was a move in a long-standing rivalry with the West; in Putin's eyes, it is Russia's most pressing strategic concern, one that predates Trump and will outlast him. Putin's Russia has to come up with ways to make up for its economic and geopolitical weakness; its traditional levers of influence are limited, and, were it not for a formidable nuclear

arsenal, it's unclear how important a world power it would be. "So, well then, we have to create turbulence inside America itself," Venediktov said. "A country that is beset by turbulence closes up on itself—and Russia's hands are freed."[25]

Washington's very inefficiency and disorganization are cards Russia will be glad to play in a game that has changed from chess (as with the Obama administration) to poker or backgammon. It could easily morph into Russian roulette. Russia's preferred weapon is not a missile or a feat of hacking; it is corruption and disorder on a global scale.

In the Western hemisphere, the proposed repeal of NAFTA (North American Free Trade Association) between Mexico, the United States, and Canada is a perfect illustration of unintended consequences of unilateral, ill-conceived "national"—i.e., mercantilist— policies.

If we take just the agricultural sector, the new closed-borders policy of the United States will hit back at the American heartland—ironically, one of the popular bastions of Trump's support. As US and Mexican food supplies are enmeshed, punitive tariffs will play havoc with supply chains. Take for example, the beef market—a subject I once studied for my analysis of Argentine development:[26] Calves raised on pastures in Mexican states are sent across the border when they turn one year old; Texas feedlots fatten them, and US packing plants slaughter them; cuts of beef are then shipped back to Mexican cities. This chain of food production and many other chains would be disrupted by protectionist policies.

If these protectionist policies come to pass, Mexicans will first suffer and then adapt. The American policies will force them to work on diversifying markets once and for all. American farmers will have even more trouble adapting to a situation that would hurt them too. An old Mexican proverb states, "*Pobre Mexico: tan lejos de Dios y tan cerca de los Estados Unidos*" ("Poor Mexico: so far from God and so close to the United States"). American nationalism will make Mexico less close to the United States. As a result, it may come, if not closer to God, certainly closer to new markets in the European Union, Asia, and Russia.

It is not just Mexico that is affected. One of the more lamentable dysfunctions of the new American protectionism is the damage it will do to hitherto well-organized and high-performance small economies, such as Australia, Canada, Chile, and Sweden.[27] As Mohamed A. El-Erian has written,

> Membership in effective international institutions brought these countries into consequential global policy discussions, while their own capabilities allowed them to exploit opportunities in cross-border production and consumption chains. But, at a time of surging nationalism, these small and open economies, however well managed, are likely to suffer.[28]

The closing of borders will also lead to degrading the collaboration on cross-border information and intelligence, and the inevitable increase in "dark networks" of organized crime and terrorism.

Refusing to act on climate mitigation and, in some cases, an ideological denial of climate change can only exacerbate the stress on the planet leading to mass human migrations.[29] On the demographic trends and the problem of carbon emissions, no exposition is clearer than that of the late Swedish statistician Hans Rosling,[30] who has been called "the salesman for the truth."

A similar latent dysfunction will result from religious zealotry and refusal to promote birth control in developing countries, which is where the explosion of populations produces migrations and violent discontent.

Another extreme example—but in the current political climate, not farfetched—is the religious, moralistic, or outright paranoid refusal of vaccination, leading to plagues and pestilence. In short, the road to hell is paved with the politics of ultimate ends and they are the most "popular" politics in our unfortunate world.

Even more troubling than any of the examples listed above, is the "hardening" of an ill-conceived *Realpolitik* among national-populist leaders—a barely disguised cult of force and messianic zeal. A convergence in style and ideas among newly elected populists and long-established dictators does not augur well for the rule of law, for effective diplomacy, or for human rights. Alliances between dictators do not last long and, sooner or later, succumb to the resort of force against each other. Opportunism and perceived profit maximization drive spurious coalitions. The relationship between Hitler and Stalin—arguably the two worst scoundrels of modern history—is an eloquent case in point. There are good and bad alliances. National-populism tends to select the bad ones—precisely because it is beholden to discrete absolutist ends and prefers case-by-case transactions. Every day I see an error chain deployed before my eyes, often with runaway consequences.

Not all error chains lead to catastrophic outcomes. For instance, a potentially *positive* unintended consequence of an *"entente cordiale"* between the presidents of Russia and the United States could very well be the reintegration—by ricochet—of a hitherto tottering European Union, provided that both Germany and France survive the onslaught of national-populism in their respective political cycles. It may make Europe great again. If they do pull through, Eurozone leaders may very well rethink their strategy. In her visit to Washington, Federica Mogherini, the European Union's foreign minister, stated that in response to the United States, Europe too would become transactional and base its approach on interests that may not coincide with those of America.[31] Europe will be more actively searching for partners beyond the United States.

If the EU survives the current political season intact, its union may well become more compact. One option would be to build a more flexible union with a "variable geometry,"[32] favored by some in the current German establishment. The alternative would be a more compact Europe, favored by some politicians in France, Italy, and Germany. Whichever path is chosen, European institutions still have the power to make it happen, especially the economic resources on which investors are betting again.[33] The new development strategy would favor greater equality, more inclusion, the repair of safety nets, and the correlative abandonment of the failed model of growth based on credit, rising asset prices, and stagnant productivity.[34] That model has reached its limits. All is left of it is widespread inequality, high unemployment, a disenfranchised young population without either jobs or assets, and rising populism.

As the triumph of national-populism in England and the United States make these two nations the site of even further inequality due to restrictive trade and migration policies,[35] the revival of a reformed Europe making use of its still robust social safety net may well change the geopolitical balance in its favor. If it comes to pass, it would be the most felicitous unintended consequence of the triumph of the extreme right in the Anglo-Saxon world.

If, on the contrary, Europe follows the nationalist trend, with anti-Euro candidates gaining power in France and other nations, then the entire continent will be fragmented, weaker, and on a path to serial, overlapping, and possibly violent conflicts. In such a scenario, a Europe of nations will face and suffer from a dramatic strategic impasse. As Martin Wolff of the *Financial Times* put it,

> Only someone ignorant of history would dream that Europe would be more prosperous, stable, influential, democratic and liberal if the EU shattered into 28 national pieces. The system of nation-states has repeatedly proved unstable. In this case, with the US increasingly withdrawn, the EU's collapse might lead to a struggle for hegemony between Germany and Russia or, worse, a pact between them at the expense of weaker neighbors. If the EU does survive, as I hope, Germany will dominate. The Germans do not want this. Why do the British?[36]

The same could be asked of the current American leadership.

Germany, the most powerful country in Europe, must avoid being caught in the middle: too big but isolated in Europe, too small for the world—as their expression goes, *Zwichen Europa und Russland* (between Europe and Russia). This is important. Despite (or perhaps because of) a terrible past, the present generation of Germans enjoys a democracy built on solid written and unwritten rules. They don't demonize rivals, and up to a point, they have accepted refugees; they prefer boredom to bombast; they don't let poorer citizens fall too far behind. Perhaps Germans can now teach Tocquevillian democracy to Americans.[37] It looks surprising and ironic that Germany may be a beacon of liberalism in the West, but it testifies to the rapidity with which positions in the geopolitical chessboard change. The German president Frank-Walter Steinmeier has said, "Isn't it wonderful that this, our difficult fatherland, is seen as an anchor of hope for many people in the world?"[38] In political as in economic development, there is sometimes a penalty for having taken the lead in old democracies like Britain and the United States, and an advantage that accrues to latecomers like Germany and Japan.[39] This is the era of reversals and surprises. Germany considers itself a responsible stakeholder and has some international clout, but it alone cannot take over from an isolationist United States the task of safeguarding the liberal world order.

If the European project falters further and the United States turns its back on the order it once sponsored, then we may face a period in geopolitics that Mark Leonard, Director of the European Council on Foreign Relations, paints with rather dark colors,

> The Internet, migration, trade, and the enforcement of international law will be turned into weapons in new conflicts, rather than governed effectively by global rules. International conflict will be driven primarily by a domestic politics increasingly defined by status anxiety, distrust of institutions, and narrow-minded nationalism.[40]

Notes

1 See "Statistical Summary of Commercial Jet Airplane Accidents, 1959 – 2015," Aviation Safety/Boeing, July 2016, www.boeing.com/resources/boeingdotcom/company/about_bca/pdf/statsum.pdf; and especially Ronald C. Kramer, "Ethics in Organizations: The Challenger Explosion," in James A. Jaska and Michael S. Pritchard, *Communication Ethics: Methods of Analysis*, 2nd ed. (Belmont, CA: Wadsworth Publishing, 1994).

2 See Juan E. Corradi, Patricia Weiss Fagen, and Manuel Garretón, eds., *Fear at the Edge* (Berkeley, CA and Los Angeles, CA: The University of California Press, 1992); and Barry Glassner, *The Culture of Fear: Why Americans are Afraid of the Wrong Things* (New York: Basic Books, 2000). In the United States today, the chances of being the victim of a terrorist attack are far lower than the likelihood of being struck by lightning or being killed by a falling vending machine. The gap between perceived and real dangers has been well studied in the social sciences, especially its utilization by fear-mongering regimes.

3 Max Weber, "Politics as a Vocation," (1919), http://anthropos-lab.net/wp/wp-content/uploads/2011/12/Weber-Politics-as-a-Vocation.pdf.
4 See Sven Eliaeson, "Between Ratio and Charisma: Max Weber's Views on Plebiscitary Leadership Democracy," Uppsala University, Disciplinary Domain of Humanities and Social Sciences, Faculty of Social Sciences, Uppsala Centre for Russian and Eurasian Studies, 1991 (English) in *Statsvetenskaplig Tidskrift*, ISSN 0039-0747, no 4, 317–339.
5 According to a 2015 study conducted by the Annenberg Public Policy Center at the University of Pennsylvania, only 31 percent of Americans can name the three branches of government (and 32 percent cannot name a single branch). In 2011, when *Newsweek* administered the United States Citizenship Test to over 1,000 American citizens, 38 percent of Americans failed.
6 Among American and other Western commentators, the current wave of right-wing populism is sometimes equated with Argentina's Peronism. If we look closer however, it is soon apparent that the quality of Perón's political judgment (despite his strategic mistakes) was infinitely superior to that of characters like Donald Trump. See, for instance, Juan Domingo Perón, *Manual de Conducción Política* (Buenos Aires: CS Ediciones, 2005). To measure the distance between Perón's and today's populisms, watch: "*Conducción Política por Juan Domingo Perón*," YouTube video, 9:03, posted on September 20, 2009, www.youtube.com/watch?v=G2srzPT3Uxg.
7 Oren Gross, "The Normless and Exceptionless Exception: Carl Schmitt's Theory of Emergency Powers and the 'Norm-Exception' Dichotomy," *Cardozo Law Review* 21 (5–6) (2000): 1825. The original formulation appeared in Carl Schmitt's *Der Begriff des Politischen* (*The Concept of the Political*), Berlin, 1932.
8 Franz Neumann, *Behemoth: The Structure and Practice of National Socialism, 1933–1944*, expanded ed. (1942, repr., Chicago, IL: Ivan R. Dee/Rowman and Littlefield, in association with the United States Holocaust Memorial Museum, 2009). Neumann used this reference to the biblical monster as a counterpart to Hobbes's Leviathan. Whereas Leviathan represents the ultimate authoritarian structure, Behemoth is, on the contrary, a form of "organized lawlessness," or a set of vested interests in confusion. Whereas in the Leviathan the subjects receive firm but clear commands, in the Behemoth compliance is no guarantee of security.
9 Cited in Gregory H. Fox and Georg Nolte, "Intolerant Democracies," 36 *Harv.Int' LL.J.* 1(1995). See also Samuel Issacharoff, "Fragile Democracies," *Harvard Law Review* 120(6) (April 2007), https://harvardlawreview.org/wpcontent/uploads/pdfs/issacharoff.pdf.

10 Philip Rucker, "Bannon: Trump Administration Is in Unending Battle for 'Deconstruction of the Administrative State,'" *The Washington Post*, February 23, 2017, www.washingtonpost.com/news/powerpost/wp/2017/02/23/bannon-trump-administration-is-in-unending-battle-for-deconstruction-of-the-administrative-state/?utm_term=.871b4d43da4f.
11 Jan-Werner Müller, "Populists Cannot Win on their Own," *Financial Times*, February 8, 2017, www.ft.com/content/69295304-ea34-11e6-967b-c88452263daf.
12 Ivan Ermakoff, *Ruling Oneself Out: A Theory of Collective Abdications* (Durham, NC: Duke University Press, 2008).
13 Zbigniew Brzezinski, *Strategic Vision. America and the Crisis of Global Power* (New York: Basic Books, 2012).
14 This is also true when, lacking an overall strategy, a government outsources its foreign policy to military commanders. Generals don't always see the big picture.
15 For an approach that combines technology, sociology, and neuroscience, see Ivan Staroversky, "The Distracted Mind with Dr. Adam Gazzaley," *StarOverSky* [blog], August 20, 2013, http://staroversky.com/blog/the-distracted-mind-dr-adam-gazzaley.
16 Manifest and latent functions are sociological concepts developed by Robert K. Merton, one of the pioneers in functional analysis in the social sciences, as early as 1938. Manifest functions are conscious, deliberate, and beneficial, the latent ones are unintended but beneficial, and dysfunctions are unconscious, unintended, and harmful. While functions are manifest or unintended, and have a positive effect on society or on some of its institutions, dysfunctions are unintended or unrecognized (latent) and have a negative effect on societal institutions. The forerunner of this analysis was Max Weber, in the aforementioned lecture on "Politics as a Vocation" (1919). Weber was addressing, with alarm, the rise of German populist nationalism in the wake of Germany's defeat in the Second World War. See also Wolfgang Schivelbusch, *The Culture of Defeat. On National Trauma, Mourning, and Recovery* (New York: Picador, 2004).
17 For the moment national-populism is more theatrical than real.
18 Geoffrey Blainey, *The Causes of War* (1973, repr., New York: Free Press, 1988). In his thorough study, Blainey argues that the common proximate cause of armed conflicts is miscalculation—a thesis that sounds simplistic, but is not.

19 For the connection between homeland authoritarianism and foreign policy disasters in the case of the Malvinas/Falklands war, see Juan E. Corradi, *The Fitful Republic*, 135–150.

20 In his *Treatise on General Sociology* (1916), Vilfredo Pareto followed Machiavelli in classifying people and especially political elites according to two basic types: lions and foxes. The "foxes" tend to be innovative, calculating, and imaginative. Entrepreneurs prone to taking risks, inventors, scientists, and philosophers fall into this category. The "lions" place much more value on duty or absolute values than on wits. They are the upholders of tradition, the guardians of dogma, and the protectors of national honor. There are of course perverse hybrids, as in Dr. Samuel Johnson's famous quip, "Patriotism [the devotion of the lions] is the last refuge of scoundrels [devious foxes]."

21 Norbert Lammert, quoted in Alison Smale, "Squeezed by Far Right, Merkel Faces a Rising Left, Too," *The New York Times*, February 13, 2017, New York edition, A7.

22 Andrew Ross Sorkin, "A Quiet Giant of Investing Weighs in on Trump," *The New York Times*, February 6, 2017, www.nytimes.com/2017/02/06/business/dealbook/sorkin-seth-klarman-trump-investors.html?_r=0.

23 Reputedly, Napoleon's advice to his marshals at a battle in 1805.

24 At stake are 49 pending trademark applications—all made during Trump's campaign—and 77 marks already registered under his own name, most of which will come up for renewal during his term. The construction-services case also raises the possibility that the president could claw back control of more than 225 Trump-related marks, held or sought by others in China, for an array of things including Trump toilets, condoms, an escort service, pacemakers, and even a "Trump International Hotel."

25 Evan Osnos, David Remnick, and Joshua Yaffa, "Trump, Putin, and the New Cold War," *The New Yorker*, March 6, 2017, 55.

26 Corradi, *The Fitful Republic*, passim.

27 Pablo Guerron-Quintana, "The Economics of Small Open Economies," *Business Review*, Q4 (2013): 9–18.

28 Mohamed A. El-Erian, "An Unstable Economic Order?" *Project Syndicate*, January 30, 2017, www.project-syndicate.org/commentary/global-economy-institutional-decay-by-mohamed-a--el-erian-2017-01?barrier=accessreg.

29 In this respect, a policy of responsibility can straddle a partisan divide. Reasonable people can legitimately disagree on the means to a common goal of climate mitigation. But a politics of "ultimate ends" between

supporters and deniers will lead humanity to a futile impasse. See the article by Martin S. Feldstein, Ted Halsted, and N. Gregory Mankiw, "A Conservative Case for Climate Action," op-ed, *The New York Times*, February 8, 2017.

30 See *The Guardian* video, 3:18, posted on May 17, 2013, www.theguardian.com/global-development/video/2013/may/17/population-climate-change-hans-rosling-video.

31 Gardiner Harris, "Europe Looks Beyond U.S. Amid a Chill Under Trump," *The New York Times*, February 10, 2017, New York edition, A10.

32 This is the idea that different parts of the European Union should integrate at different levels and pace depending on the political situation in each individual country.

33 Europe has been faring better than the United States in the latest indices of economic surprises.

34 Corradi, *Why Europe? The Avatars of a Fraught Project*. In my book, I have analyzed the unsustainable nature of this model.

35 Even in Brexit England and Trump's America, when the real consequences of nationalist policies begin to bite, the populist tide may turn. The white working class who delivered Brexit in the UK and Mr. Trump to the White House may wonder if they have been taken for a ride. After all, how many times can one expect turkeys to vote for Thanksgiving?

36 Martin Wolff, "Brexiters Must Lose If Brexit Is to Succeed," *Financial Times*, March 28, 2017.

37 This is the provocative argument of Simon Kuper, "What Germany Can Teach the US about Democracy," *Financial Times Magazine*, February 8, 2017.

38 Quoted in *Der Spiegel*, February 11–12, 2017.

39 The term is Thorstein Veblen's in his book *Imperial Germany and the Industrial Revolution* (1915). For a more recent and comprehensive version of the thesis, see Mancur Olson, *The Rise and Decline of Nations* (New Haven, CT: Yale University Press, 2011).

40 Mark Leonard, "What Liberal World Order?" Project Syndicate, February 28, 2017, www.project-syndicate.org/commentary/trump-brexit-liberal-world-order-by-mark-leonard-2017-02?barrier=accessreg.

References

Blainey, Geoffrey. *The Causes of War* (1973, repr., New York: Free Press, 1988).

Brzezinski, Zbigniew. *Strategic Vision. America and the Crisis of Global Power* (New York: Basic Books, 2012).

"*Conducción Política por Juan Domingo Perón*," YouTube video, 9:03, posted on September 20, 2009, www.youtube.com/watch?v=G2srzPT3Uxg.

Corradi, Juan E. *The Fitful Republic* (Boulder, CO: Westview Press, 1985).

Corradi, Juan E. *Why Europe? The Avatars of a Fraught Project* (Amazon e-Book, Opinion Sur, 2013).

Corradi, Juan E., Patricia Weiss Fagen and Manuel Garretón, eds. *Fear at the Edge* (Berkeley, CA and Los Angeles, CA: The University of California Press, 1992).

El-Erian, Mohamed A. "An Unstable Economic Order?" *Project Syndicate*, January 30, 2017, www.project-syndicate.org/commentary/global-economy-institutional-decay-by-mohamed-a--el-erian-2017-01?barrier=accessreg.

Eliaeson, Sven. "Between Ratio and Charisma: Max Weber's Views on Plebiscitary Leadership Democracy," Uppsala University, Disciplinary Domain of Humanities and Social Sciences, Faculty of Social Sciences, Uppsala Centre for Russian and Eurasian Studies, 1991 (English) in *Statsvetenskaplig Tidskrift*, ISSN 0039–0747, no 4, 317–339.

Ermakoff, Ivan. *Ruling Oneself Out: A Theory of Collective Abdications* (Durham, NC: Duke University Press, 2008).

Feldstein, Martin S., Ted Halsted and N. Gregory Mankiw. "A Conservative Case for Climate Action," op-ed, *The New York Times*, February 8, 2017.

Fox, Gregory H. and Georg Nolte. "Intolerant Democracies," 36 *Harv.Int' LL.J.* 1(1995).

Glassner, Barry. *The Culture of Fear: Why Americans are Afraid of the Wrong Things* (New York: Basic Books, 2000).

Gross, Oren. "The Normless and Exceptionless Exception: Carl Schmitt's Theory of Emergency Powers and the 'Norm-Exception' Dichotomy," *Cardozo Law Review*, 21(5–6) (2000): 1825.

Guerron-Quintana, Pablo. "The Economics of Small Open Economies," *Business Review*, Q4 (2013): 9–18.

Harris, Gardiner. "Europe Looks Beyond U.S. Amid a Chill Under Trump," *The New York Times*, February 10, 2017, New York edition, A10.

Issacharoff, Samuel. "Fragile Democracies," *Harvard Law Review* 120(6) (April 2007), https://harvardlawreview.org/wpcontent/uploads/pdfs/issacharoff.pdf.

Kramer, Ronald C. "Ethics in Organizations: The Challenger Explosion," in James A. Jaska and Michael S. Pritchard, *Communication Ethics: Methods of Analysis*, 2nd ed. (Belmont, CA: Wadsworth Publishing, 1994).

Kuper, Simon. "What Germany Can Teach the US about Democracy," *Financial Times Magazine*, February 8, 2017.
Lammert, Norbert quoted in Alison Smale. "Squeezed by Far Right, Merkel Faces a Rising Left, Too," *The New York Times*, February 13, 2017, New York edition, A7.
Leonard, Mark. "What Liberal World Order?" *Project Syndicate*, February 28, 2017, www.project-syndicate.org/commentary/trump-brexit-liberal-world-order-by-mark-leonard-2017-02?barrier=accessreg.
Müller, Jan-Werner. "Populists Cannot Win on their Own," *Financial Times*, February 8, 2017, www.ft.com/content/69295304-ea34-11e6-967b-c88452263daf.
Neumann, Franz. *Behemoth: The Structure and Practice of National Socialism, 1933–1944*, expanded ed. (1942, repr., Chicago, IL: Ivan R. Dee/Rowman and Littlefield, 2009).
Olson, Mancur. *The Rise and Decline of Nations* (New Haven, CT: Yale University Press, 2011).
Osnos, Evan, David Remnick and Joshua Yaffa. "Trump, Putin, and the New Cold War," *The New Yorker*, March 6, 2017, 55.
Pareto, Vilfredo. *The Mind and Society. Treatise on General Sociology*, 4 vols. (New York: Dover, 1963).
Perón, Juan Domingo. *Manual de Conducción Política* (Buenos Aires: CS Ediciones, 2005).
Rosling, Hans. *The Guardian* video, 3:18, posted on May 17, 2013, www.theguardian.com/global-development/video/2013/may/17/population-climate-change-hans-rosling-video.
Rucker, Philip. "Bannon: Trump Administration Is in Unending Battle for 'Deconstruction of the Administrative State,'" *The Washington Post*, February 23, 2017, www.washingtonpost.com/news/powerpost/wp/2017/02/23/bannon-trump-administration-is-in-unending-battle-for-deconstruction-of-the-administrative-state/?utm_term=.871b4d43da4f.
Schivelbusch, Wolfgang. *The Culture of Defeat. On National Trauma, Mourning, and Recovery* (New York: Picador, 2004).
Schmitt, Carl. *Der Begriff des Politischen (The Concept of the Political)* (Berlin: Duncker & Humblot, 1932).
Sorkin, Andrew Ross. "A Quiet Giant of Investing Weighs in on Trump," *The New York Times*, February 6, 2017, www.nytimes.com/2017/02/06/business/dealbook/sorkin-seth-klarman-trump-investors.html?_r=0.

Staroversky, Ivan. "The Distracted Mind with Dr. Adam Gazzaley," *StarOverSky* [blog], August 20, 2013, http://staroversky.com/blog/the-distracted-mind-dr-adam-gazzaley.

"Statistical Summary of Commercial Jet Airplane Accidents, 1959 – 2015," Aviation Safety/Boeing, July 2016, www.boeing.com/resources/boeing dotcom/company/about_bca/pdf/statsum.pdf.

Veblen, Thorstein. *Imperial Germany and the Industrial Revolution* (1915, repr., London: Kitchener, 2003).

Weber, Max. "Politics as a Vocation," (1919), http://anthropos-lab.net/wp/wp-content/uploads/2011/12/Weber-Politics-as-a-Vocation.pdf.

Wolff, Martin. "Brexiters Must Lose If Brexit Is to Succeed," *Financial Times*, March 28, 2017.

8
WHEN NOBODY MINDS THE SHOP

A 2,400-year-old text has a wealth of advice for citizens and leaders in societies that are today still rationally organized; the words of wisdom are very appealing but difficult to follow in practice because of institutional degradation and bad popular habits.

In his famous book on strategy, compiled 20 centuries ago, the Chinese Master Sun Tzu warned of certain risks that can befall even the strongest powers. In this chapter, I will dwell on two of his central prescriptions that have special utility in the geopolitical context of the twenty-first century, and their contemporary relevance confirms the judgment of many that *The Art of War* is a text for the ages.[1]

Since the 1980s, the *Sunzi* (Sūnzǐ bīngfǎ)—as *The Art of War* is also called—moved beyond the realm of security studies to the campuses of business schools and seeped into popular culture around the world, magnified by social media. But let us not get distracted by the book's fame and its multiple applications, good or bad; instead let us focus directly on those two prescriptions.

One prescription for a strong state—that is, a state with strong armed forces—is to avoid protraction. A large section of the *Sunzi* is concerned with the dangers and costs of protracted operations. Protraction poses a mortal danger to all belligerents, from which no one benefits, or rather, from which all lose.

Looking at the map, it is clear that the Middle East—which some prefer to call the Levant—is an area of protraction *par excellence*, with conflicts that have been raging for decades, nay centuries, and tend to have expanded and multiplied. From the colonial drawing of boundaries after the First World War, to the continued redrawing during and after the Second World War, to the insertion of the state of Israel in 1948, to the many wars—Iran, Iraq, Kuwait, the Sinai, and so on—since then, to the failed Soviet invasion of Afghanistan, to the fiasco of American intervention in Iraq, to the current civil and sectarian wars on multiple fronts, to the failure and collapse of several states, to the many awakenings and ensuing nightmares, the Levant is home to protraction—what is regularly referred to as "endless war."

For any great power to intervene directly in an area of acute protraction is to court failure or worse—direct and embarrassing defeats. It happened to all great powers, and the list is long: the British Empire, France, Russia, Japan, and the United States, to name a few that got—repeatedly—a bloody nose.

Current globalization adds new ingredients to the explosive mix: speedy interaction and spillover—features that have been present before in protracted conflicts, but on a smaller scale and at a much slower pace (think of the international brigades in the Spanish Civil War). Today, there is an active network of warriors, weapons, information, ideology, propaganda, and recruitment spanning large areas of the world with astounding speed.

Under such circumstances, only containment is the appropriate strategy, keeping a firm list of priority interests in the region (e.g. access to energy sources, free navigation routes, etc.) and securing them through a series of temporary and opportunistic alliances with a variety of actors. Containment is a policy to prevent the spread of a rival ideology and/or socio-economic system in the global chessboard. It represents a middle-ground position between appeasement and rollback. In a context of protraction, there are no friends and no safe allies—only nimble, cynical, and shifting dealmakers who preferably are at a distance or work through proxy actors on the scene of "endless war." Patience is paramount, persistence essential, good intelligence uppermost. The use of non-obvious and non-lethal levers of influence (financial tools for example), and the capacity to shift gears on short notice all play their part.

But none of these features of protraction avoidance plays well in an open society, in the full light of public and social media. Especially in the case of the United States—still the most powerful nation on Earth—the populace has been habituated to expect decisive battles, to support "just wars," and to honor heroes. It is Hollywood's war. This is a serious hindrance to the pursuit of appropriate strategies and leads us to another central principle of strategy in the work of Master Sun.

This prescription of the *Sunzi* puts emphasis on the intellectual, as opposed to the heroic, qualities of statesmanship and command. The intellectual qualities enable the leadership to see the "large picture," and lead the country in the deployment of the appropriate instruments of action. This quality is what Master Sun called "net assessment." In fact, there is a Director of Net Assessment at the US Department of Defense, whose task is to uncover lessons that may be of value to the production of American strategies.

What is meant by the term "net" or "strategic assessment?" In general, it implies an analysis of the *interaction* of two or more national security establishments—usually oneself and a potential enemy—both in peacetime and in war.

Net assessment is divided into several categories, the most salient one being what Master Sun calls "the spiritual strength of the state," by which he means the ability to mobilize, make sacrifices, and to resist the rivals' attempt at subverting its resolve. The other categories—environment, terrain, command, and method—are very important but may come to naught with the failure of the first.

It has repeatedly been said that democracies are slow to rally around a security threat, yet when they finally do, they display unstoppable momentum. Their spiritual strength is kept in reserve. When needed, it is deployed in massive ways. This feature was shown several times during the twentieth century, most especially in reference to the United States.

However, in the twenty-first century, we live in an age of what a political scientist has called "post-democracy." In fact, democracy in the rich countries has devolved into a plutocracy with entertainment for a consumerist base. If Victorian England was derided in the nineteenth century as "a nation of shopkeepers,"[2] America in the twenty-first could well be called "a nation of shoppers,"[3] who has outsourced defense to professionals and contractors—and, increasingly, to robots—in far-away places. That is fertile terrain for warring actors in a zone of protraction to goad the containing power into direct intervention through a series of more or less spectacular provocations (i.e., terrorist acts), which play on the fears of pacific consumers. The common and ultimate goal of terrorists is twofold: to draw the big power into a protracted fight in their terrain; and to effect "regime change" in the homeland of the powerful, from an open society into a garrison state, turning Athens into Sparta.

In the remote period of Chinese history when the *Sunzi* was written, command was no longer based on aristocratic pedigree; it was an intellectual enterprise, based on the ability to test and process the elements of net assessment and to craft a strategy with their subtle variations. In our own days of post-democratic dysfunction in politics (in fact a period of widespread political *reaction* in Europe, Russia, and the United States), instead of proper command as the *Sunzi* instructs, leadership could fall into the hands of mediocre politicians, of hot-headed advisors who prefer bombast to cold strategy, and with a frightened populace behind them, ready to endorse cockamamie "crusades." If that day should arrive, then even the greatest powers will meet their demise.

The Swamp: A Middle Eastern Version of Strategic Depth

From a historical point of view, the conflagration of the Middle East—Syria, Iraq, Libya, Afghanistan, Palestine, and Iran, among other participants—does not offer an analogy with other periods and it is not a paragon. It is something worse. Categorically, I would say it is a continuation.

Consider the following tale:

> It is the summer of 1943, in southern Italy.
> "*E la Guerra, ¿continua?* (And the War, does it continue?)" an oddly dressed-up sailor asks a peasant on the shores of Sicily. He was up in the conning tower of an old submarine that had just emerged from the depth of the Messina Straits.

The peasant looks at him in astonishment and replies, "*Si, la Guerra continua* (Yes, the War continues)."

"*Ah, maledetto Káiser!* (Oh, the goddam Kaiser!)" the commander shouts in frustration, and the vessel re-submerges again.

This is one of many jokes that circulate about the Italian Navy. Here the humor lies in the confusion between the First and Second World Wars. The submarine emerges in the middle of the second war but belongs to the first one. She has been hiding since 1918.

When reviewing the current situation of the Middle East the joke is not funny anymore. In these days, a baroque coalition orchestrated by the United States has besieged the city of Mosul, in Iraq, which has been under the dominance of the so-called Daesh "caliphate" (Islamic State).[4] The siege was long, the fight ferocious. The Iraqi army, helped by special US forces in their rearguard, aimed at displacing the Islamic activists and eventually occupying the city. The siege coalition was formed by Kurd shock troops and Shiite militias trained by Iran. As the population of Mosul is mainly Sunni, there is a well-founded fear of possible retaliations and revenge by Shiite militias. In this intermingling of crossed interests and occasional alliances, the United States places itself once more in a strategic impasse, which has been the constant of its intervention in the Middle East. On the one hand, they coordinate the attack, and on the other, they try to mediate among the components of their own coalition. The Mosul siege evokes the siege of Troy narrated by Homer, where the Greek coalition is permanently threatened by internal disputes. In the case of Mosul, other references are worth citing. Daesh warriors not only offered a fierce resistance, but also employed a "scorched-earth" tactic to deny the future conquerors the fruits of their victory. Here we are reminded of the Russian strategy against Napoleon's invasion.[5] Meanwhile, the civil population that had suffered the harsh Islamic imposition of the caliphate is now being used as a human shield and is trapped in the crossfire. As in Aleppo, the civilians of Mosul were literally cannon fodder.

On top of that, Turkey has decided to intervene in the conflict—though no one requested its intervention. Turkey has two main objectives: one is to hold back the initiative of Kurdish soldiers, as the Kurdistan nation looks to install its own state in an area occupied today by Iraq, Iran, and Turkey.[6] Under the pretext of attacking the caliphate, the Turks want to attack the Kurds. The second Turkish objective is to limit the growing regional influence of Iran and its influence in Baghdad.

What is most striking is the justification for Turkey's involvement offered by Recep Tayyip Erdogan, the Turkish president (who does not deny his aspirations of being a new sultan). Erdogan has already settled Turkish troops at Bashiqa base in northern Iraq, and now insists on participating in the Mosul battle. Thus, Turkey intends to turn into the defender of Turkemos and the Sunnite Arabs who live in and around the city. Let us remember here that Turkey is still a full NATO member, which complicates the geopolitical chessboard. The Turkish president is flirting with Russia and China—something weird for a NATO member—and, in this way, he helps to internationalize the situation even more.

In his rise to personal dictatorship, President Erdogan invokes the "historical injustice" of the First World War, when triumphant allies divided the Ottoman Empire in the Middle East and artificially created the presently troubled countries of Iraq, Libya, Syria, Lebanon, and Palestine. The memory of the Great War is very vivid in these countries because it reconfigured the Middle Eastern map with the remains of the Ottoman Empire that had once been an ally of Kaiser Wilhelm II of Germany, whom Great Britain and France had defeated. These powers signed controversial agreements upon which the new independent states were founded. The project of a great, united Arab state, governed by Faisal, son of Mecca's Sharif, promptly cracked under the schemes of London and Paris governments.

The Sykes-Picot agreements of 1916 were contorted, as the colonial ambitions of the UK and France frequently clashed. One of the main architects of the treaty, the British colonel-diplomat Mark Sykes proposed splitting the territory between Great Britain and France with a line in the sand that ran from the Mediterranean city of Saint John of Acre up to Kirkuk in Mesopotamia. In the international Versailles conference of 1919 and then the Geneva one, the English mandate received backing with regard to what is now Iraq and Jordan; and the French mandate received support about Syria and Lebanon. Georges Picot,

France's representative, de-coupled Lebanon's territory from Syria, to which Palestine was united in the beginning.

Aleppo and Mosul share the same history and culture. Mostly Sunnite, both cities were part of the Zengid state in the twelfth century. They split after the collapse of the Ottoman Empire when the Western powers divided up the spoils of the First World War. The French wanted Mosul to be part of Syria, but the English objected and Mosul ended up as part of Iraq. Over time, both cities turned rebellious—in one case against the fierce dictatorship of the Alawite minority in Syria and in the other case, more recently, against the Shiite oppression entrenched in Bagdad.

To quote Turkish president Erdogan, "We have never voluntarily accepted the frontiers that were imposed on our country." Nothing would please him more than being able to redraw those frontiers.[7]

In this way the US troops try to build a compromise among the warring factions in their own coalition: Turks, Kurds, Sunnites, Shiites, Iraqis, and Iranians. But the Americans are in a tight corner—or as the Argentine country saying states, they are as confused as "a dog caught in a game of bocce."[8]

Let us now think of the Middle East as today's equivalent of the Balkan states in 1914[9]—countries about which Churchill said, "produce more history than they can consume"—and the frontiers established by the Western powers in 1918 as being contested once more. The conclusion is obvious: in this region, the First World War has not ended. After a long strategic sabbatical, it is exploding again—though with different nuances, accents, and actors. If Sarajevo was the spark that ignited such conflagration, now a whole region of the planet sparks and burns—as in those days—with huge and unsuspected possible consequences. We could go further. First, Second, and Third: wouldn't they be just a long, bloody single war? Unpredictability in all capitals—Washington, Moscow, Ankara, and in some European countries—fans the flames, and can be the prelude to a global conflagration.

In the meantime, in this war that is spreading like wildfire, many children are dying. In Aleppo, Russians and Alawites bomb schools. In Mosul, kids are trapped in the crossfire between the savagery of Daesh and the guns of the great army, which surrounds the city. If and when they "liberate" it, they will start fighting each other. But a wounded or dead child in Aleppo is no different than a child killed or wounded in Mosul, or to another drowned at sea. Today, an entire generation of children has been robbed of their young lives in terror. Their small wrecked bodies weigh tons on the conscience of the world.

The week of September 25, 2016, is a date that will live in infamy. A short cease-fire, agreed upon between the United States and Russia, ended in Syria and gave way to a resumption of ferocious hostilities. That same day, an aid convoy from the United Nations was hit by an air strike, which the Americans and Europeans blamed on the Russians. Meanwhile, the Bashar-al-Assad regime mounted a massive offensive on eastern Aleppo—a holdout of rebels that are fighting that regime. As in the past, the regime used barrel and cluster bombs as well as chemical weapons indiscriminately against the population. The attacks on civilians constituted a clear breach of international humanitarian law. The air attack was the deadliest in a conflict that has lasted five and a half years, claimed 300,000 lives, and driven half the country's population from their homes. Eventually what was left of Aleppo fell to the troops of Mr. Assad.

This massacre brings back the memory of Guernica during the Spanish Civil War, in April of 1937 (ironically, in those days Soviet Russia sided with the "good guys"—the Republican government—against Franco). Under the code name Operation *Rügen*, it was an aerial bombing of the Basque town of Guernica, carried out at the behest of nationalist rebels by their allies—the Nazi German Luftwaffe's Condor Legion and the Fascist Italian *Aviazione Legionaria*. The attack involved the deliberate targeting of civilians by a military air force. The number of victims is still disputed, but it hovers around 1,000—a small figure by comparison with the repeated aerial attacks on the Syrian city of Aleppo.

In response to these attacks, and commissioned by the Republican government of Spain at the time, the great Spanish artist Pablo Picasso composed a mural-sized oil painting on canvas. Picasso used a palette of gray, black, and white, and his work remains one of the most eloquent anti-war paintings of all times. *Guernica* was first exhibited in Paris in 1937. By the express will of the painter, the work remained outside Spain until the end of the Franco regime. From 1985 to 2009, a tapestry copy of the masterpiece was displayed on the wall of the United Nations Building in New York City, at the entrance to the Security Council room. One wonders what the current members of the Security Council might think of the subject matter today as they head into their fruitless deliberations on the Syrian crisis.

The responsibility for the present crimes lies not only with the regime of Mr. Bashar-al-Assad and the supporting government of Russia, but also with the misguided strategy of the Western powers led by the United States. Why was the Western policy in Syria wrong?

During this crisis, the United States insisted on a premise that few if anybody believed in—that there was no military solution to the Syrian conflict—and to which the Russians paid lip service. The consummate Russian diplomat Sergei Lavrov took the hyperactive-but-less-effective American Secretary of State John F. Kerry down the proverbial garden path of arch diplomacy to a dead end. Ultimately, the United States and its allies simply had to give up—as was clear in their remarkable joint statement, "The burden is on Russia to prove it is willing and able to take extraordinary steps to salvage diplomatic efforts."

The initial premise of Western strategy cited above ended in failure. In any conflict, this happens when one of the parties in dispute wrongly arrives at the conclusion that the fight has reached an impasse, whereas the other side does not believe so and continues to advance. To be sure, the eventual objective—but only eventual—is a series of diplomatic agreements to settle the Syrian civil war by negotiation and compromise.

On such misguided premise, the United States believed that Russia would be willing to pursue a negotiated settlement in return for a ceasefire and the alleged prestige of conducting joint military operations with the United States in Syria against terrorist groups. That was wishful thinking, and it was easily debunked.

The Russian view, on the other hand, was the opposite, and it was no secret. Sergei Lavrov said it loud and clear that President Bashar-Al-Assad was the only viable partner in the fight against "terrorism"—a very flexible epithet, since my freedom fighter is your terrorist, and vice-versa. Lavrov called Assad's army the single most efficient force fighting terror in Syria. For the Russians, the strategic goal is: let Assad prevail, bloody as his "victory" will be (but then, the Russians never blinked at unbounded brutality under Stalin who was reported to have said, "death solves all problems—no man, no problem."), and only then, try to come to terms with Assad and convince him to be more "civilized."

It is a strategic mistake to appease Russia in the hope of its future collaboration in stabilizing the Middle East. The onus should be put on the Putin regime to improve relations. Combatting Daesh is not the Russian objective; instead, it is to keep the Assad regime in power. Russian offers of air assets rather than troops are not what the West needs, but a coordinated plan to retain the ground initiative, in consultation with Europe. Unfortunately, a Eurosceptic administration in Washington can only advance Russian strategic objectives to the detriment of the West. Mixed signals on all sides will only prolong the Syrian agony and the instability in the region.

The belief that negotiations under a cease-fire would produce peace and some sort of transition to a post-Assad regime, together with the half-baked and contradictory policies of the US on the ground, placed America in a strategic pickle. Exhortations against such massacres without action to stop it did and will do nothing at all.

Erroneous strategic assumptions on the part of one world power, and opportunistic intervention on the part of rival powers fuel the fires of the Middle East. When nobody minds the shop, the fires will burn indefinitely. Trapped in the deadly conflict, the civilians as was mentioned before, continue to be cannon fodder in vast numbers. They die in many horrible ways. America doesn't suffer; Russia doesn't suffer; Turkey doesn't suffer in this carnage, while Europe bears the brunt of a refugee burden on its eastern and southern flanks.

Notes

1 http://classics.mit.edu/Tzu/artwar.html.
2 "L'Angleterre est une nation de boutiquiers."—Napoleon I (attributed to) See www.theguardian.com/money/2006/oct/23/careers.theguardian7.
3 "I encourage you all to go shopping more."—George W. Bush, the president's news conference on December 20, 2006, www.presidency.ucsb.edu/ws/index.php?pid=24389.
4 The Islamic State of Iraq and the Levant (ISIL)—known on some occasions as the Islamic State of Iraq and Syria (ISIS) or as Daesh—is an insurgent

terrorist group of wahhabi jihadist character formed by loyal militants of Abu Bakr al-Bagdadi who, in June 2014, auto-proclaimed the caliphate from the Iraqi city of Mosul, demanding loyalty from every Muslim in the world.

5 Not very different were General Sherman's scorched-earth tactics in the American South. In South America, General Manuel Belgrano also used this tactic in the Argentine war of independence. In a strategic retreat, called the Jujeño exodus, the population of Jujuy and Salta provinces was forced to withdraw to Tucuman, and the Argentine troops swept away everything that could serve the Spanish Realist Army in their path.

6 About 6 million Kurds, a distinctive ethnic group with its own language and culture, different from Arab, Persian, and Turkish populations that prevail in that zone, inhabit an autonomous area of 40,000 square kilometers in the northern part of the country. They represent 15 percent of the Iraqi population and most of them are Sunnite Muslims, but they tend to adopt a less conservative interpretation in terms of preserving faith, which brought upon them the rejection of extremist Muslim groups.

7 In addition the geopolitical interests of Turkey and the US are rapidly diverging, ending what used to be a stable partnership born in the Cold War. Erdogan's "new Turkey" is far more concerned with the perceived threat from Kurds in Iraq and Syria than it is about ISIS. It supports Hamas, Lybian militias, the Muslim Brotherhood in Egypt, and finally, challenges NATO by flirting with Russian weapons. A time might come when America and its allies in Europe will show Turkey the door in their military alliance. See Philip Gordon, "Turkey and the US Face the End of a Promising Partnership," *Financial Times*, October, 11 2017, 9.

8 The literal translation is "like a dog in a bocce court," meaning confused, lost.

9 A note of caution is apt in this context. The fragile "solution" to the breakup of Yugoslavia in 1998 is about to unravel and risks turning the Balkans into another powder keg.

References

Bush, George W. The President's News Conference on December 20, 2006, www.presidency.ucsb.edu/ws/index.php?pid=24389.

Gordon, Philip. "Turkey and the US Face the End of a Promising Partnership," *Financial Times*, October 11, 2017.

Napoleon I. "Who are you calling a shopkeeper, Napoleon?," www.theguardian.com/money/2006/oct/23/careers.theguardian7.

Tzu, Sun. *The Art of War* (New York: Barnes & Noble, 2004).

9
GEOSTRATEGIC RIVALRIES IN A PERIOD OF POTENTIAL DEGLOBALIZATION

The slowdown in Chinese growth (from 10 percent to 6 percent of annual GDP) incites commentaries in the Western press regarding a "crisis" in this Asian country. In light of the crisis of the Western social, economic, and political system, the Chinese stagnation mitigates the spiritlessness among Western elites. Largely, such interchange involves a projective defense mechanism, which Freud once used to study. Two in distress make sorrow less, the saying goes.

The reality is different: China is transforming from a factory with a cheap labor force, exporting surpluses throughout the world, to a modern society of services and innovation, focused on better domestic living standards with sustainability. Challenges are huge but are no match to the Western impasse. Certainly, there are motives for worrying in the West, including the fact that China's change accelerates the current crisis in Europe and decreases US world power. Latin American countries must also adapt to this new reality.

The Chinese have a popular curse that is as old as the Middle Kingdom. It goes, "May you live in interesting times." There is bad news though; we have entered a very interesting historic period for the West—and China is at the center of the geopolitical field.

As described above, the prevailing globalization model is cracking. Neo-liberalism had to abandon its promises—in particular, free trade and financial imperialism are being whipped all over the place. At the same time, the systems that opposed it are breaking down. Among the great powers, US recklessness in foreign policy threatens to diminish its hegemony in the Middle Eastern quicksand. That region's implosion accelerates the rupture of the European Union. The opportunism of middle powers—Russia, Turkey, and Iran—encourages the regional disequilibrium in the Mediterranean. Germany is losing control over Europe, and Europe, in turn, is rapidly losing its ability to act together. Africa, which retains a great development potential, is impeded by intertwined tribal conflicts and, above all, by the colonial aftermath and the interests of central countries to have access to the continent's natural resources. Latin America vacillates between two failures: that of ultra-neoliberalism and the electoral foundering of popular-based governments that sought to correct those excesses, albeit in superficial ways. The country that weighs more in the region—Brazil—is still not able to overcome an acute governability crisis. With few exceptions, all these countries stumble today at the rhythm of the tango "*Los Mareados*" ("The Doped Ones").[1] Frankly, it is far from a promising picture.

In many regions of the world, we will have to live with the resurgence of protectionism, reactionary nationalism, and an adventuresome foreign policy. We know that the tendency toward self-absorption, "staying at home," "living within our means," and caring only about "people like us" (likeminded people and from the same upper class segment) is unviable and a multiplier of conflicts. But that is the most likely reaction in the short and medium terms.

In this inward race only three countries are capable of leading, because of their geographic location, the size of their internal market, and their resources (natural, technological, and human), and because of their strategic depth in terms of security: the United States, the People's Republic of China, and the Russian Federation. For the reasons I expose in this book, neither the United States nor Russia is able to react creatively to the aforementioned globalization crisis. The United States suffers from both an external strategic impasse and an internal political impasse, which delay the arrival of a new phase in economic and social development. The Russian Federation is not able to compensate the deindustrialization that succeeded the collapse of the Soviet Union with a model dependent on the export of natural resources. In this chapter, I will focus on examining the perspectives for the third country of the geopolitical troika: China.

In my view, only China is seriously addressing the challenge of changing its model of economic growth, keeping the global profile in every sector as much as possible but at the same time, shifting toward an economy with a different composition of its GDP. I risk saying that, compared with other strong countries, China is a pioneer now. Its strategy today is directed toward a service economy with a more advanced and innovative technological profile. In particular, I follow the essays from a Brazilian sociologist Anna Jaguaribe.[2]

For 30 years, the Chinese economy grew at an annual average rate of 10 percent—quite a record in the world's economic history. I dare say that this large country has entered a third phase in its development. The first one—under the communist system sponsored by Mao—was, to my understanding, the historical equivalent of what Marx called the phase of primitive accumulation. The second—under Deng Xiaoping's sponsorship, experienced with state capitalism and foreign investment—poured out the productive surplus toward exports. During that phase, China changed into the world's industrial workshop. In global terms, its growth can be summarized as follows: with cheap labor, an ultra-industrialization for exports. It entailed the deindustrialization of a good part of the capitalist mature economies that moved toward a specialization in services, especially financial services and avant-garde technology in terms of communications and information.

Having reached this point, as every economy that matured before, China faces a "natural" deceleration of growth, with the need to give more emphasis to the internal market, a more extensive redistribution of wealth toward the working class, and to provide more services to the whole population and encourage greater consumption. In brief, the country is in the middle of a process of "export substitution," with a correlative import substitution of industrial inputs—that is, a larger internalization of the productive chains. China's state-backed programs in science and technology have acquired a more civilian orientation.

If it were successful, the Chinese program would mark a shift from a copycat manufacturer using borrowed or stolen technology to one that sets the pace of innovation. No longer will Chinese tech companies—like Alibaba,[3] Baidu,[4] and Tencent[5]—ape Google or eBay. Instead new "national champions" in areas like semiconductors will lead the field. In many ways the strategy is one of smart autarky. The Mercator Institute for China Studies, based in Germany, maintains that the policy aims of obtaining control of the most profitable segments of networks and supply chains in the global economy. The Chinese leadership understands that technological innovation is one of the pillars that will sustain its superpower status. By comparison, Western political trends toward autarky seem defensive and even regressive.

If China becomes the master of its own technology, its rise to superpower status will continue—barring a war. Instead of copying ready-made technology from the West, China has embarked on a series of programs to borrow Western models that advance technological goals, notably Germany's Industrie 4.0.[6] It shifts manufacturing away from cheap labor-intensive industries to smart industries, including cloud computing, big data, robotics, and full automation.[7] Western governments will try to block these developments and denounce them as "unfair," but their strategies can be bypassed—not least by Western high-tech multinationals, which can accommodate China. In case it is prevented from investing in the West's high-tech sectors, China is preparing a counter-strategy of setting up its own research centers, even with the help of such "global research universities" like NYU-Shanghai, through joint-venture schemes. Moreover, at a time when Americans are making budget cuts in the area of advanced science research, China might even sponsor a new "brain drain"—this time in reverse. For example, the new "Made in China" program features the establishment of 19 national data labs.[8] The scheme is no different than the transfer of soccer players or star sailors from other countries to hot spots of excellence in the Chinese territory. Once nurtured by the state, the technological hubs of China will eventually acquire a life of their own. Huawei already holds the world's biggest number of patents.[9] Other Chinese companies, flush with cash, are busily buying patents right and left. In short, we are witnessing an eastward shift in the locus of innovation. We should not be surprised if the world's first quantum computer is invented in China—like gunpowder once was.

This change is as revolutionary and disruptive as the previous ones, but with an important novelty. This time, the world's economic relations, which took for granted the previous global division of labor, is altered. The economies—so far the recipients of the Chinese industrial surplus with all their commercial and financial links tied to this model—are forced to adapt in order to enter a new phase of productive competition with China, to experience an even larger fall in their own (already low) rate of growth, and to suffer the consequences, such as the end of the super-cycle of commodities. The current Chinese transition represents a true shake-up for the rest of the world—including all emerging markets.

As Jaguaribe mentions, after 30 years of an accelerated catching up, China is entering a new phase and, thus, faces disequilibria and disarticulations from their previous accelerated growth on the one hand, and from transformations in the global economy on the other.

China answers the first challenge with the so-called strategy of a "New Normal" (larger internal modernization) and the second one with the strategy called the "New Silk Route." They are policies designed for bringing sustainability to the economic model, with a new combination of globalized market economy and state intervention in new key sectors and with a new investment profile. It is a dynamic version of "living within their means." In foreign policy, Chinese strategy aims at an intensification of commerce, investments, and economic arrangements with other Asian countries, and a more active inter-regional presence.

The two larger strategic lines reinforce each other within a general plan of turning from the catching-up phase to an innovation economy. The authorities of the single party (transformed into a managerial state-party) want to deal with social and economic problems in a global context but without the advantages that characterized the previous phase of growth. For many observers, it is a major reform in the financial, tributary, and administrative systems, thus fostering the internal market, with innovation as the motor of growth.

It is about a reorientation of investments with deceleration of growth in an uncertain international context. This choice implies a larger concentration of the central power (more personalized and less collegiate under President Xi Jinping) to break the internal resistances from the interests created in the previous phase (anti-corruption campaigns to heal the bureaucracy and change the profile of the military-industrial sector). Hence, we face a great debate on the future of the system, its solidity or fragility, the crossed resistance from inside and outside, and the trust and legitimacy of the managing and control apparatus.[10] We do not yet know which ways of participation, predictability, and new institutions will come out of this process. I do insist: we live in times truly interesting.

The rise of China in the last decades transformed global conditions for development of the emerging economies and the conditions for sustainability in mature economies. The current reform in China will transform them again. One thing is true: the global geopolitical axis is inexorably moving toward the East, where China has gone from being an exception to becoming its own rule. Whatever the outcome of this new transition, the rest of the world will not be the same as we know it.

In summary, we may say that the model, which today is reaching its limits, was characterized by a spectacular growth that transformed the economy into the world's manufacturing center and a crucial link in the global productive chain. The main characteristics of the model were: long-term strategic planning, high savings and investment rates, a financial system composed by public banks to facilitate infrastructure works and lend credit to large state companies, and competitive insertion of Chinese enterprises into the world market. Among the facilitating factors, we must note the favorable demographic curve—cheap energy and labor force—and repressed demand.

Over time, the model accumulated several disequilibria such as indebtedness and over-investment at the provincial level, financial speculation, and high corruption. The current reform wants to correct the course, change the incentives, repress corruption, and eliminate the volatility of the stock exchange.

The change toward a "New Normal" aims at lowering quantitative growth indexes and increasing qualitative growth indexes; going from an excessively exporter profile to a service economy geared toward the internal market, and achieving environmental improvements (development of alternative energies). In fiscal terms, the Chinese are trying to mitigate the region's debt and redirect credit toward the private sector. In institutional and legal terms, they are searching for more transparency and predictability.[11]

In terms of foreign policy, from now on, China will try to extend its direct investments, sponsor multilateral funds, and achieve more density in regional agreements. The final objective might be the internationalization of the renminbi as the currency of reference.

Without going into further details, we can say that China is currently focused on the systematic search for new economic opportunities and new comparative advantages. That is more than what can be said of Europe and the United States regarding their economies, which, in comparison, seem very dis-oriented.

As a final note, I will say that in the context of global stagnation and crisis China is at the forefront of innovation. The sun rises in the East, though sometimes we do not realize it due to the cloudy skies and isolated thunderstorms of the West. As for these cloudy skies I will indulge in a far-flung fantasy more as a provocation than as a prediction.

The State of the Unions: A Strange Lesson from Europe for the United States

For years now, I have been writing on the hows and whys of the European Union as a fraught project.[12] To sum up my arguments in the vernacular: the European project was a half-baked cake that had it been completed according to the recipe would have been very good. The ingredients were attractive and seemed sensible: tight integration was needed if the continent was to manage an economically divergent monetary union; to strengthen defense cooperation; and to remain credible as both a trading bloc in the face of other—older and emerging—powers, and a strong defense league when confronted with assertive neighbors, notably Russia and Turkey. The EU also needed a common strategy vis-à-vis the massive migrations from Africa and the Middle East. However, as the Italians say, "*Tra il dire e il fare c'è di mezzo il mare.*" ("Between saying and doing is the sea.").

The recipe was excellent but impossible. The treaty that was needed to construct such union (like the American Constitution once wisely followed the Articles of Confederation) was unrealistic and resisted by the various countries that formed the EU. And so the cake remained half-baked and did not taste good to anyone who sampled it. What to do then? How to get out of the impasse? As in cooking, the best solution is to start over again. Yes: repeal and replace. To some, that may sound paradoxical, but Brexit shows the way.

The way out of the impasse is to accept a process of disintegration, followed by reintegration. As Wolfgang Münchau wrote in an article for the *Financial Times*, "The EU as constituted is monolithic. It is stuck with a legal framework for everybody that suits nobody."[13] When—not if—that framework collapses, the best way to start building a new framework would be to design a variable structure. In Münchau's words, it would be

> a structure with a reasonably integrated core, surrounded by a less integrated outer layer. All member states would be part of a customs union and the single market but not necessarily the single currency or the interior and foreign policy apparatus.[14]

In other words, it would be a federation of countries with a core and a periphery, with different speeds and different options.

If the breakup of the European Union is an impending possibility, then what about the larger world outside its borders, and in a more distant future?

Science fiction moves ahead of the scholarly scenarios. Free from the constraints of serious disquisition, science fiction projects a future beyond the current impasse, but one worth perusing, if only for a moment—and if only to gauge the paucity of present-day established discourse. In *The Diamond Age*,[15] the author Neal Stephenson refers to a future (a few decades hence) when nanotechnology has transformed much of life. The book posits that in the near future (circa 2050), most nation-states will have broken down and given way to the creation of "phyles" as the major form of social and political organization.

In Stephenson's book the various religious, ethnic, racial, cultural or economic groups within a country—which have become too big, too "diverse," and too "inclusive"—want to get out. As travel and the

Internet become universal, people start to realize that they may have very little in common with their countrymen, and a lot more in common with people who may be on the other side of the globe—many of whom will feel the same way about their own countrymen.

In this fantasy, the nation-state will be a dinosaur; it will no longer make sense in a world with today's technology and demographics, and will break down into smaller post-national affinity groups.

Perhaps the vision is not outlandish. Perhaps the first round of the process began when the USSR broke into 15 nation-states, Yugoslavia into six, Czechoslovakia into two, and Sudan into two as well. Europe would be a candidate for round two, as it fragments into a looser federation with "variable geometry." And others may follow.

My own geopolitical contribution in this context is that of an *agent provocateur*. It is a radical projection. What if the United States of America—which today is polarized and fractured socially, culturally, and geographically—became also a more flexible, variable-speed structure, with a dynamic and tightly integrated core, based primarily but not exclusively on the two coasts of the continent, and a less integrated outer layer, in need of different policies, protection, and also assistance from the core? It sounds ironic: the core is actually the outer, i.e., the coasts, while the outer layer is the center. This outer layer would be primarily but not exclusively composed of rural areas, deindustrialized towns, and districts with relatively immobile populations in need of special efforts to re-join the Union—including foreign investment by countries like China.

The American Union would not be monolithic—though it would be tighter at its core. Outer-layer states would not be monolithic either; they would have the right, but not the obligation, to join core policy areas. The core areas would have the right but not the obligation, to accept them back. The reverse of such greater flexibility in the Union would be this: the outer-layer states would not have the ability to define the policies of the whole United States through the current and obsolete constitutional capacity of over-representation—the very process that led to the presidency of Donald J. Trump.

Should such design come to pass, the United States of America will have become an American Federation. It would be a symmetrical completion of the end of the Cold War. Just as the Union of the Soviet Socialist Republics was replaced by the Russian Federation, the American Federation would succeed the United States of America. The difference being that America will have what Russia lacks: innovation, economic dynamism, and social experimentation. All three exist under the umbrella of freedom. Without fake solutions and demagogues on top, only then would America be great again—but it would be a very different America from the one we have lived in so far.

Notes

1 *"Los Mareados"* ("The Doped Ones"), song lyrics, https://letrasdetango. wordpress.com/2012/02/07/los-mareados/.
2 Anna Jaguaribe, *"Desafios da Economia Chinesa Hoje."* Notes based on discussions and interviews during the annual monitoring program of the Chinese economy organized by the Institute for Brazil-China Studies/ IBRACH in partnership with Tsinghua University in Beijing, June 2016.
3 Alibaba is China's biggest online commerce company.
4 Baidu, Inc. is a Chinese language Internet search provider.
5 Tencent is a leading provider of Internet value-added services in China.
6 See Heiner Lasi, Hans-Georg Kemper, Peter Fettke, Thomas Feld, and Michael Hoffmann, "Industry 4.0," *Business & Information Systems Engineering* 6, (4, 2014): 239–242; and Prof. Dr. Henning Kagermann *et al.* "Securing the Future of German Manufacturing Industry." trans. Joaquín Blasc and Dr. Helen Galloway. Final Report of the Industrie 4.0 Working Group, National Academy of Science and Engineering/Acatech, Munich, Germany, April 2013, www.acatech.de/fileadmin/user_upload/Baumstruktur_nach_ Website/Acatech/root/de/Material_fuer_Sonderseiten/Industrie_4.0/ Final_report__Industrie_4.0_accessible.pdf.
7 See the reports of the Mercator Institute for China Studies, 2016 and 2017, Berlin, Germany, www.merics.org/en.
8 "Made in China 2025" "is an initiative to comprehensively upgrade Chinese industry," www.csis.org/analysis/made-china-2025.
9 Huawei Technologies Co. Ltd. is a Chinese multinational networking and telecommunications equipment and services company.
10 Regarding this debate, also see The Editors, "The Governance of China," NYR Daily, *The New York Review of Books*, March 13, 2016, www.nybooks. com/daily/2016/03/13/governance-china-conference/?utm_medium= email&utm_campaign=NYR%20Pinckney%20Weerasethakul%20

China&utm_content=NYR%20Pinckney%20Weerasethakul%20 China+CID_cb2b209fee08d0e39703254b5c46ac2f&utm_source=Newsletter&utm_term.
11 See Hu Angang, "Embracing China's New Normal," *Foreign Affairs*, May/June 2015, www.foreignaffairs.com/articles/china/2015-04-20/embracing-chinas-new-normal. Readers can find more details on this model in the nine directions presented at the 2015 Economic Conference of the Central Committee of the Chinese Communist Party.
12 Corradi, *Why Europe? The Avatars of a Fraught Project* (2013, Amazon e-Book).
13 Wolfgang Münchau, "A Multi-speed Bloc Offers Europe a Future," *Financial Times*, March 12, 2017, www.ft.com/content/f01f1266-058e-11e7-ace0-1ce02ef0def9.
14 Münchau, "A Multi-speed Bloc."
15 Neal Stephenson, *The Diamond Age* (New York: Bantam Books, 1995).

References

Angang, Hu "Embracing China's New Normal," *Foreign Affairs*, May/June 2015, www.foreignaffairs.com/articles/china/2015-04-20/embracing-chinas-new-normal.

Corradi, Juan E. *Why Europe? The Avatars of a Fraught Project* (2013, Amazon e-Book).

Jaguaribe, Anna. "*Desafios da Economia Chinesa Hoje.*" Notes based on discussions and interviews during the annual monitoring program of the Chinese economy organized by the Institute for Brazil-China Studies/IBRACH in partnership with Tsinghua University in Beijing, June 2016.

Kagermann, Henning Prof. Dr. *et al.* "Securing the Future of German Manufacturing Industry," trans. Joaquín Blasc and Dr. Helen Galloway. Final Report of the Industrie 4.0 Working Group, National Academy of Science and Engineering/Acatech, Munich, Germany, April 2013, www.acatech.de/fileadmin/user_upload/Baumstruktur_nach_Website/Acatech/root/de/Material_fuer_Sonderseiten/Industrie_4.0/Final_report__Industrie_4.0_accessible.pdf.

Lasi, Heiner, Hans-Georg Kemper, Peter Fettke, Thomas Feld and Michael Hoffmann, "Industry 4.0," *Business & Information Systems Engineering* 6, (4 2014): 239–242.

"*Los Mareados*" ("The Doped Ones"), song lyrics, https://letrasdetango.wordpress.com/2012/02/07/los-mareados/.

"Made in China 2025," www.csis.org/analysis/made-china-2025.

Mercator Institute for China Studies, 2016 and 2017, Berlin, Germany, www.merics.org/en.

Münchau, Wolfgang. "A Multi-speed Bloc Offers Europe a Future," *Financial Times*, March 12, 2017, www.ft.com/content/f01f1266-058e-11e7-ace0-1ce02ef0def9.

Stephenson, Neal. *The Diamond Age* (New York: Bantam Books, 1995).

The Editors, "The Governance of China," NYR Daily, *The New York Review of Books*, March 13, 2016, www.nybooks.com/daily/2016/03/13/governance-china-conference/?utm_medium=email&utm_campaign=NYR%20Pinckney%20Weerasethakul%20China&utm_content=NYR%20Pinckney%20Weerasethakul%20China+CID_cb2b209fee08d0e39703254b5c46ac2f&utm_source=Newsletter&utm_term.

Epilogue

This book began with a poem by W.B. Yeats. It ends with a poem by Percy Bysshe Shelley. In between these two poems, I sought to identify the social forces that put our world at risk: a risk of many and endless wars, a risk of human and natural resource depletion, and a risk of losing a stable future. In particular, I tried to identify the dangers that lurk for the international order that America shaped, and the prospects for a different order, built with other powers.

I tried to stay away from predictions, and focus instead on possibilities, good and bad—from the standpoint of my values.

As I was writing the book, the very linchpin of the present order—the United States—took what I consider a turn for the worse, toward internal decay and external aggression. One possible solution is for the country to find a more sensible path. The management of relative geopolitical decline need not be—literally—the end of the world. Another is to follow the current road leading to a scary impasse.

If the present administration in Washington survives the chaos it has provoked and manages to hold on to power, then its fate—and ours—might be that of Shelley's king, as in his well-known poem, *Ozymandias*, which merits another recitation:

> I met a traveller from an antique land
> Who said: "Two vast and trunkless legs of stone
> Stand in the desert . . .

> Near them, on the sand,
> Half sunk, a shattered visage lies, whose frown,
> And wrinkled lip, and sneer of cold command,
> Tell that its sculptor well those passions read
> Which yet survive, stamped on these lifeless things,
> The hand that mocked them, and the heart that fed:
> And on the pedestal these words appear:
> 'My name is Ozymandias, king of kings:
> Look on my works, ye Mighty, and despair!'
> Nothing beside remains.
> Round the decay
> Of that colossal wreck, boundless and bare
> The lone and level sands stretch far away."[1]

May the poet's vision not come to pass. As darkness seems to be falling upon the world in which I grew up, I can only express hope by quoting a call, sometimes made at a gathering of Jewish people in France, to raise their glasses and drink together in honor of precious life: *Pour que le pire cesse d'arriver*.[2]

Notes

1. Percy Bysshe Shelley, *Ozymandias*, 1818, www.poetryfoundation.org/poems/46565/ozymandias.
2. May the worst cease to happen.

Postscript

After Pax Americana: Ten Theses on Geopolitical Disarray

As in a kitchen, if asked to boil down the arguments and narratives of this book into a thick sauce, the reduction (in Italian the word is *colatura*) would consist of ten theses. They track closely the sequence of the chapters:

Thesis 1

We are witnessing the rapid undoing of the post-Second World War international order, without a replacement yet in sight. The scale of planetary problems demands global and concerted solutions. These solutions are presently visible and persuasive, but they are non-enforceable.

Thesis 2

Prediction does not work because it cannot anticipate events. Only the formulation of plausible scenarios will help actors adapt and manage unanticipated events.

Thesis 3

The death knell of late capitalism is the loss of a non-capitalist context. Left to its own triumphant devices, the system is likely to self-destruct.

Thesis 4

Just as late or "compleat" capitalism tends to self-destruct, so do systems that seek to replace their roots and branches. Assembling a new mixed system, with a specified hierarchy of components and the appropriate sequence of policies, will be the task of the future.

Thesis 5

When a social hierarchy loses credibility and a convincing rationale, it is likely to be overthrown.

Thesis 6

With the advancement of technology, the manipulation of minds is both extreme and inter-personal (participatory). Total alienation turns into a new form of false subjectivity. Its main characteristic is distraction. There are remedies for this dysfunction.

Thesis 7

The West ruled for three centuries, but its unity is breaking up and its purpose is breaking down. This decline has been silent for a number of decades, but it has become strident now. Attempts to retrieve the past are the wail of groups upon whom history is about to roll.

Thesis 8

Like switch points in a railway network, certain decisions have long-term consequences, which become clear often only in retrospect. On the basis of past experience, it is possible to gauge the implications of actions that are guided more by emotions than by sound discernment. The current wave of national-populism will destroy rational strategic choice. This leads to the democratic self-destruction of democracies.

Thesis 9

Correct strategy consists of two opposite and symmetrical rules of avoidance: one is avoidance of rash military action; the other is avoidance of protraction in conflict. These rules are as old as the art of war itself. They can be ignored, but at great peril for states and blocs of states.

Thesis 10

Barring catastrophic war, Eastern powers will emerge from the present geopolitical disarray as the guarantors of a different international order. In the new concert of nations and regions, the West will be allowed to play an important but secondary role.

Index

2 degree centigrade target 5
abdications 101
Accabadora, La (Murgia) 84
　Accabadora
accabadors 82–93
Africa 129
agency 14
aging 28–29
agrarian reforms 38–39
'Aleph, The' (Borges) 15
Aleppo 121, 123–124
alliances between dictators 106–107
American Federation 136–137
amoral familism 83
Ancien Régime 50–51
Arbatov, G. 26
Archimedes 12, 77
Argentina 44–45, 59
Aristotle 3–4
Art of War, The (Sun Tzu) 117
artificial negativity 27
Ash, T.G. 62
Asian Infrastructure Investment Bank 89, 103
Assad, B. al- 124, 125–126
attainable consensus 7–10
Augustine, St 17
Augustus, Emperor 92
austerity policy 61
Australia 106
autarky 131
authoritarian leaders 75; alliances between 106–107

authoritarianism tempered by incompetence 99–100
automation 27
avoidance: of protraction 117–120, 143; of rash military action 120–126, 143

balance of terror 1
Bannon, S. 101
Bauman, Z. 44
beef production 105
Berlusconi, S. 90
Borges, J.L. 15
Brazil 129
Brexit 62, 84
business 23–25, 30–31, 33
butterfly effect 12–15

Caesar, Julius 82, 91–92; imagined letter to Octavius 92–93
Caesarism 91
Cameron, D. 84, 87
Canada 106
capitalism 1, 10–11; compleat 28, 55–56, 62–63; crises 44; end of 22–35, 142
carbon emissions 3–6
carbon tax 9–10
case-by-case decisionism 100, 102
Castro, F. 38, 42–43
Cavafy, C.P. 85–86
centralization of control 38–40
Chaos Theory 12
charisma 38
Chile 106

China 29, 56–58, 88, 89, 103–104, 128, 129–134
Christianity 17
Churchill, W.S. 16
civil society 63
civilians, attacks on 124
class structure 59–60
climate change 2–6, 10, 106
collective action 7–10
competitive elitism 91
compleat capitalism 28, 55–56, 62–63
complexity 15–16
computer business systems (CBSs) 24
confusion, rule by 100–101
Conley, D. 43–44
consensus: American bipartisan 22–23; attainable 7–10; cosmopolitan 17
containment 118
control: centralization of 38–40; of the workforce 73–74
cooperation 7–10
cooperatives 45
corruption 104–105
cosmopolitan consensus 17
critical social theory 25
Cuba 16, 36–43; revolution 37–39
cultural values 53

Daesh caliphate (Islamic state) 121
Dalio, R. 52
Davos summits 51–52
debt 29–30
defeasance in the West 81–96, 143
deglobalization, potential 128–139, 144
Deng Xiaoping 130
Diamond Age, The (Stephenson) 135–136
digital technology 44; propaganda 70–80, 143
disintegration 135–136
disorder 104–105
disproportion 11–18
distraction 17–18, 82–93
distributional conflicts 30

economic stagnation 40
education 32; and combating propaganda 72–73; political 98
elites 50–69, 143
elsewhere society 43–44
emergency plans 6
empires 91
entente cordiale 23

equalization 38–40
Erdogan, R.T. 122, 123
Erian, M.A. El- 106
Ermakoff, I. 101
European Union (EU) 61, 85, 107–108, 129; disintegration then reintegration 134–135; multiple crises 16; risk of disintegration 8–9
exceptional situations 100
export substitution 57, 130

fake news 71
Farage, N. 62, 84
fascism 59
fear of terrorist attack 98
financial crisis of 2008 30, 60–61
financial sector 45, 61
First World War 14, 122–123
fitness 14
flexible, variable-speed structure 136–137
food supplies 105
fragmentation 82–93, 135–137
France 50–51, 87, 122–123; National Front 62
Francis, Pope 36
Franz Ferdinand, Archduke, assassination of 14
freedoms 31
Friedman, T. 57

Germani, G. 58–59
Germany 87, 108–109; Nazism 100
gig economic platforms 73–74
global institutions 1, 3
global problems 1–21, 142
global warming 2 degrees target 5
globalization 14–15, 101–102; paradoxical effects 75
Goebbels, J. 100
good society 30–33
grassroots initiatives 44–46
Great Depression 54
Greece 84–85
Grillo, B. 87
growth: China 29, 130; decline in rate of 29
Guernica 124–125
Guernica (Picasso) 124–125

Hacker, J. 32
Hardin, G. 7–8
Hayek, F. 27
Head, S. 23–24

health insurance 32
healthcare 2–3, 45
historical fatigue 40–42, 43
Hitler, A. 101, 107
Hollande, F. 87
human trafficking 29
Hungary 62
hurricanes 12
Husserl, E. 85

immanence, and transcendence 17
immigration 61
individualism 43
industrial speed-up 74
inequality 30, 51–55, 57, 63, 73, 107–108
Inglehart, R. 53
innovation 130–134
insecurity 24, 73
intellectual property rights 104
intraviduals 43–44
Iraq 121–122, 123–124
Islamic state 121
isolationism 102–103
Italy 81, 82–83, 86–87; joke about the Italian navy 120–121

Jaguaribe, A. 130, 132
Janus 29–30
Jordan 122

Kaku, M. 28–29
Kerry, J. 125
Kissinger, H. 58
Klarman, S. 103
Kotkin, J. 54
Kurdistan 121–122

large technology companies 76–77
late capitalism 22–35, 44, 142
Latin America 129; *see also under individual countries*
Lavrov, S. 125
Le Pen, M. 62, 87
Lebanon 122–123
left-wing politics 60
leftist political movements 62
Leonard, M. 109
limited purpose banking (LPB) 45
local community self-organization 44–46

Macmillan, H. 11
Macron, E. 87

'Made in China' program 131
manipulation of minds 70–80, 143
Mankiw, G. 10
Mao Zedong 130
Marathon, battle of 13, 16
Marcuse, H. 30–31, 40–41
markets 31; vs states 2–6
Marx, K. 27
McCain, J. 103
Merkel, A. 87
Merton, R.K. 53
Mexico 105
Middle East 118, 129; strategic depth 120–126
military action: avoidance of protraction 117–120, 143; avoiding rash action 120–126, 143
military expenditure 55
Mill, J.S. 9, 77
Mogherini, F. 107
monitored aspirations model 5–6
mortgage mutual funds 45
Mosul 121–122, 123–124
motivation 74
Münchau, W. 135
Murgia, M. 84

NAFTA 105
Napoleon Bonaparte 103–104
nation-states 75; end of 135–136
National Front 62
national-populism 97–116, 143
National Socialism (Nazism) 100
nationalism 11, 62, 75–76; fragmentation and strategic distraction in Europe 82–93
NATO 89, 122
negative externality 9
net assessment 119–120
Netherlands, The 85
Neumann, F. 100
'New Normal' policy 132–134
'New Silk Route' policy 132–133
noblesse oblige 53–54
Norris, P. 53

Obama, B. 36, 61
Octavianus (Augustus) 92
Odysseus 27, 33
Ostrom, E. 7
Ottoman Empire 122, 123
'Ozymandias' (Shelley) 140–141

INDEX

Paestum 81, 90
Palestine 122, 123
Papandreou, G. 84
Paris agreement on climate change 3–6, 10
particularism 32–33
peer review 5
Péron, J.D. 54
Peronism 59
Petain, Marshal 101
phantasmagoria 72
'phyles' 135–136
Picasso, P. 124–125
Piketty, T. 51
planetary problems 1–21, 142
planetary sovereignty 7, 8
plebiscitary leader democracy 98
Poland 62
political education 98
political judgment 98
Polyphemos 27
population growth 4, 106
populism 11, 52–54, 59; national-populism 97–116, 143
populism index 52
post-democracy 119–120
potential deglobalization 128–139, 144
precariat 24–25, 58, 73
prediction 142; strategy and predictability 11–18
preparedness 14, 16–17
primary social mobilization 59
primitive accumulation 130
privilege 50
productivity 17–18
propaganda 70–80, 143
protectionism 102–106
protraction, avoidance of 117–120, 143
Putin, V. 104

racism 62
rash military action, avoidance of 120–126, 143
rationality 38
referenda 98–99
reintegration 135–136
religion 17
Renzi, M. 87
repression 39–40
resistance 26
right-wing political movements 62
risk, shifted 31–32

Roman empire 23, 27–28, 81–82, 91–93
Rome, republic of 81, 91–92
Roosevelt, F.D. 54
Rosenthal, E. 2
Rosling, H. 4, 106
Ross, C. 45
Russia 56, 88, 89–90, 104–105, 107, 129–130; and the Middle East 124, 125–126; *see also* Soviet Union

Sardinia 83–84
Schumpeter, J. 27
Schmitt, C. 100
Schwartz, B. 7
science fiction 135–136
secondary social mobilization 59
secular stagnation 55
Shelley, P.B. 140–141
Sicily 83
Sieyès, Abbé 50, 51, 63
sin 17–18
smart autarky 131
social media 44, 59; propaganda 70–80, 143
social mobilization 59–60
socialism 10–11, 36–49
Socrates' dialogues 73
sovereignty 8; planetary 7, 8
Soviet Union 26, 40, 41, 136; *see also* Russia
Spain 85
Spanish Civil War 124
spiritual strength of the state 119
Stalin, J. 107
state socialism 10–11, 36–49
states: vs markets 2–6; sovereignty 8
Steinmeier, F.-W. 108–109
Stephenson, N. 135–136
Stiglitz, J. 51
strategic vision 17, 98
Summers, L. 55
Sun Tzu 117, 119
Sweden 106
Switzerland 16, 51–52
Sykes-Picot agreements 122–123
Syria 122–123, 124–126
Syriza 62, 85

technological approach to climate change 6–7
technological giants 76–77

technological innovation 130–132
Telos 25
ten theses on geopolitical disarray 142–144
terrorism 120; fear of terrorist attack 98
Tertullian 72
Third Estate 63
Tilly, C. 51
Tocqueville, A. de 50–51
totalitarianism 70, 77
tragedy of the commons 3–4, 7–10
Trans Pacific Partnership (TPP) 103
transcendence, immanence and 17
trente glorieuses, les 22–23, 54
tropical storms 12
Trump, D. 36, 61, 82, 88–90, 103–104, 136
Turkey 121–122
Turkle, S. 44, 73

uncontested power 26, 55–56
unintended consequences 105, 107–108
United Kingdom (UK) 62, 122–123; Brexit 62, 84
universal insurance program 32
universal protection 32
unmanageable surplus 55

vaccination 106
Varoufakis, Y. 85
Venediktov, A. 104–105
Venezuela 40
Vietnam 16
Vietnamese way reforms 41–42

'Waiting for the Barbarians' (Cavafy) 85–86
Washington State Initiative 732 10
Weber, M. 13, 98, 100
Weimar Republic 100
Wilders, G. 85
Williams, J. 92–93
Wolff, M. 108
workforce, control of 73–74
working class 24, 60
World War I 14, 122–123

xenophobia 62

Zaslavsky, V. 41
Zuckerberg, M. 76

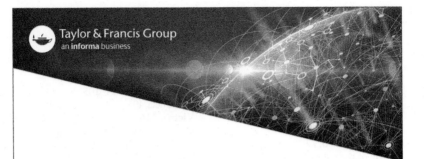